AF457850

THE BISON PRINCIPLE

PRAISE FOR THE BISON PRINCIPLE

"For too long, local governments have confused growth with progress and expansion with success. In *The Bison Principle*, Jamie Sabbach applies a clear-eyed fiscal lens, reminding us that maintenance before expansion, honest lifecycle math, and disciplined leadership are the foundations of long-term resilience. This book challenges public servants to build systems their communities can afford to sustain."

- Charles Marohn
Founder & President, Strong Towns

"If you are looking for a book that confronts the inconvenient truths in local government, *The Bison Principle* delivers. With raw honesty, it challenges how we think about fiscal responsibility and disciplined decision-making. More than a compelling read, it is a practical resource for how municipal systems should build, pay for, and protect community quality of life."

- Sara Hensley
City Manager (retired), City of Denton, Texas

"*The Bison Principle* explores the uncomfortable realities facing municipal systems throughout the United States, while exposing the widening gap between community expectations and fiscal constraints. Its message is important as we prepare the next generation of local government leadership to serve with courage, intention, and eyes on the future."

- Julie S. Knapp, Ph.D.
Director, Indiana University Executive Development Program

"*The Bison Principle* offers clarity and resolve in the moments leaders need it most. It names the fiscal realities many inherit, but few are prepared to confront, clarifies the scope of financial challenges, and outlines practical steps toward sustainability. For those willing to face hard truths and chart a responsible path forward, this book is a steady guide and a clear call to action."

- Erika Strojinc
Executive Director, Buffalo Grove (IL) Park District

"In *The Bison Principle*, Jamie Sabbach thoughtfully weaves history, professional insight, and personal storytelling into a compelling reflection on leadership, stewardship, and the responsibility we carry as public servants. Her perspective goes beyond budgets and balance sheets, reminding us that true sustainability includes how we protect our physical assets, our time, our resources, and the public trust."

- Stephanie Stephens
Executive Director, California Park & Recreation Society

"*The Bison Principle* isn't a book of comfort; it's a book of clarity. It examines where we've been, how we got here, and the hard truths we must confront about our decisions and resolve. It reminds us that the future of our communities rests with each of us."

- Nathan Ullyot
Director, City of Reno (NV) Parks & Recreation

"*The Bison Principle* provides an engaging analysis of both the causes and consequences of short-sighted fiscal decisions. It compels us to shift the narrative, confront financial realities, and pursue strategies to promote sustainable budgetary decisions for future generations."

- Andrew J. Mowen, Ph.D.
Professor, The Pennsylvania State University

"Optimism. Tenacity. Clarity. Purpose. Judgement. *The Bison Principle* outlines the ingredients for good governance. It also challenges us to demonstrate these attributes and, in doing so, build systems that serve our communities for generations to come. In sharing the lessons she's learned from decades of public work and private practice, Jamie is showing that in her heart, she's a teacher. I am grateful for another opportunity to learn from her through this book."

- Ali Rhodes
Municipal Park and Recreation Director and Advocate

THE BISON PRINCIPLE

CLARITY, DISCIPLINE, AND COURAGE IN LOCAL GOVERNMENT THROUGH THE LENS OF PARKS AND RECREATION

BY JAMIE SABBACH

110%, INC.

Written by Jamie Sabbach

Printed in the United States of America
First Printing: April 2026

ISBN (hardcover) 979-8-9942081-0-6
ISBN (paperback) 979-8-9942081-1-3
ISBN (ebook) 979-8-9942081-3-7
ISBN (audiobook) 979-8-9942081-2-0

Library of Congress Control Number: 2026906516

For bulk purchases or to hire author Jamie Sabbach to speak at your event, visit 110percent.net/the-bison-principle
or email info@110percent.net

The most expensive line item
in local government
is avoidance.

And avoidance compounds.

CONTENTS

FOREWORD

by Alexis Hermosillo
Mayor of the City of El Mirage, AZ

There is something deeply human that draws people into public service.

For many of us, it begins with a simple love for people and place. A belief that life should feel fuller and more connected where we live. That children should have somewhere safe to play and explore. That neighbors should have spaces to gather. That the everyday moments that make up a life should feel supported by the community around them.

And then, slowly, another reality reveals itself.

In government, especially in local government, even our most hopeful ideas must pass through the limits of a budget. Every program, every park, every promise carries a cost that must be sustained year after year. The truth is that happiness and quality of life can only stretch as far as the systems that support them. It is not a cynical realization. It is a humbling one.

Parks and recreation sit right in the middle of that

tension. They are where quality of life becomes visible — opportunities for self-expression and adventure, where belonging is shaped, and where we breathe a little easier at the end of a long day. These spaces preserve what nature has given us and create room for community to grow. In many ways, they are the quiet backbone of healthy and thriving communities.

But caring for that backbone requires something from us. It requires honesty about what things cost. It requires discipline to sustain what we build. And it requires leaders who are willing to follow conviction rather than fold under the pressure of politics.

Anyone who has served in public life knows that these decisions are rarely simple. The instinct to say yes is strong. The pressure to avoid disappointment is real. Yet leadership asks us to hold two truths at once — the love we feel for the people we serve, and the responsibility to steward resources wisely so that what we build today can still exist tomorrow.

The Bison Principle speaks directly to this tension with clarity and care. The message is both practical and deeply philosophical: fiscal stewardship is not about scarcity. It is about respect. Respect for community. Respect for the professionals who maintain these systems. Respect for the generations who will inherit the choices we make.

Human progress is often measured in grand ideas and sweeping change. But much of it begins closer to home. It begins in our parks, our neighborhoods, and the spaces where people come together. Leadership, in many ways, begins in our own backyard.

So the question becomes not whether we want thriving communities. Of course we do. The real question is how we care for them. How we protect what matters. How we lead with both heart and discipline.

This book invites us to think deeply about those questions.

And more importantly, to answer them with courage.

- Alexis Hermosillo
  Mayor of the City of El Mirage, AZ

INTRODUCTION

For more than a century, public parks and recreation existed for a clear purpose: to support human well-being. Early systems were modest, local, and woven into daily life. They offered simple public spaces that strengthened connection, belonging, and community health. In doing so, parks and recreation became one of the most tangible expressions of local government.

This book is about parks and recreation and the broader local government systems that fund and shape them. Because these services are deeply valued and highly visible, they are often where the gap between community expectations and organizational capacity becomes most apparent.

Over the past several decades, that gap has widened. As cities expanded, parks and recreation followed a pattern of development characterized by larger facilities and longer travel distances to reach them. Mega sports complexes and regional recreation centers became symbols of progress. Many remain well-loved by those who use them, yet their scale and sprawl created fiscal expectations that operating budgets were never designed to support. Maintenance was deferred. Costs compounded.

And despite decades of pursuing major projects often justified under the banners of "public health," "access," and "economic development," health and well-being continued to decline, inequity persisted, and local economies remained vulnerable.

This all raises a basic question: Who has this model truly served?

After years of building bigger and farther out, many communities are acknowledging the need to recalibrate—less about expansion, more about reinvestment. Progress now means strengthening what people use every day: parks closer to home, trails linking neighborhoods to schools and parks, plazas that invite activity and conversation, and adaptable multi-use play areas. These investments deepen connection, reinforce public life, and don't require endless capital campaigns. What they do need is clarity of purpose, disciplined decision-making, and the courage to rethink long-held assumptions.

Everything in this book has been shaped by time spent inside public systems and by the work of 110% Inc., where we inspire decisions that are ethical, courageous, and financially sustainable across parks, recreation, and other quality-of-life services.

We've stood with organizations and communities

across the country as they confront the same unavoidable tension: wanting more than they can afford and making promises they can't afford to keep.

PART I - FOUNDATIONS

THE GROUNDING

Bison survive storms not through speed or force, but through grounding—staying oriented, conserving energy, and moving with intention when the weather turns.

It is the accumulated wisdom of when to move, when to hold, and how to remain aligned when conditions change. Without grounding, even the strongest herd is exposed.

The same is true of the public systems that support quality of life. Purpose gives them meaning, but meaning alone does not sustain them. When quality of life is treated as abstract or assumed, the structures beneath it quietly weaken.

Grounding requires reflection on why these systems exist, how they came to be, and what realities they must face.

What is not grounded in understanding, values, and limits cannot endure.

CHAPTER 1
CLARITY, DISCIPLINE, AND COURAGE

> "In any moment of decision, the best thing you can do is the right thing; the next best is the wrong thing; the worst thing you can do is nothing."
>
> – Theodore Roosevelt

More than twenty years ago, I moved to the Mountain West. At first, it was the beauty that struck me—the vastness, the peaks, the silence, and the way light moved across the high alpine desert. Over time, though, it wasn't the mountains or forests that captivated me the most, but the openness between them—the meadows where life endures through wind, scarcity, and change.

In that openness, survival is not accidental. Plants adapt low to the ground. Animals conserve energy, move deliberately, and endure long seasons of uncertainty. Over time, I began to notice that some species don't just survive this landscape; they embody it.

The bison predates our institutions, our grids, our optimism, and our declines. Before there were governments, subdivision covenants, capital plans, or ballot initiatives, there were bison on this land. They endured ice ages, colonization, eradication campaigns, and industrialization. And they are still here.

They are massive animals—thousands of pounds of bone, muscle, and dense fur built to withstand brutal cold, relentless wind, and long periods of scarcity. Their strength is not ornamental; it is functional, evolved for survival in some of the harshest conditions on the continent.

Their endurance is not explained by physical strength alone; it is also behavioral. When storms rise, cattle turn and run with them, prolonging their exposure. Bison do the opposite. They lower their heads and charge directly into the storm. They get through it faster, not because they enjoy hardship, but because they understand something essential about it: storms cannot be outrun, only faced.

That instinct is not romance. It is resolve. It is design. It is wisdom earned through centuries of survival.

And it's a principle. And it's the principle this book is built on.

Public systems, especially in parks, recreation, and quality-of-life services, stand in a storm of their own. Costs rise faster than revenues. Expectations outpace the willingness to pay. Deferred maintenance grows into a structural deficit. Each postponed decision makes the next one harder, until the weight of inaction becomes its own kind of crisis.

And yet this is when leadership matters most. To right-size, confront reality, enforce policy, and design for endurance rather than approval—this is what public service looks like at its best. It was never meant to be easy work. It was meant to build systems that benefit society, strong enough to withstand disruption.

For decades, local governments have expanded faster than they have learned how to sustain. We have built new things with optimism and deferred their maintenance with indifference. We have treated growth as progress and affordability as permanence. But things have changed. What once felt manageable now feels precarious.

The Bison Principle calls for a different kind of leadership—one grounded in fiscal stewardship rather than sentiment. It begins with truth: understanding what things actually cost, what the public is willing to pay for, and what must be protected, especially when the decision may not be popular. It requires a hard stop on pretending that every service can be delivered at yesterday's prices or that doing more with less is a strategy. It isn't. It's exhaustion disguised as virtue.

Facing the storm means accepting accountability for our choices, our budgets, and our promises. It means rejecting the comfort of "later" and the illusion that someone else will carry the burden. Like the bison, it means facing what lies ahead.

This book is organized around three qualities that separate organizations that endure from those that don't.

Clarity.
Clarity is shared understanding. It is the ability to say—plainly and consistently—what we mean, what we are doing, and why. Clarity turns instinct into intention. Without clarity, everything becomes negotiable. Clarity is what makes responsible decision-making possible before money is spent and promises are made.

Discipline.
Discipline is follow-through. It is what happens after clarity—when we translate what we say we value into the structures that protect it. Discipline is the willingness to hold the line when pressure shows up. Discipline is about consistently doing what matters.

Courage.
Courage is choosing responsibility. Courage is telling the truth. It is disappointing people today in order to protect tomorrow. Courage means refusing denial as a strategy. Courage is acting early enough that the storm doesn't become a permanent operating condition.

These aren't abstract ideals. They are imperatives.

A Call to Action

Fiscal stewardship is a civic responsibility. It is how we say to the next generation: *We cared enough to plan with you in mind.* When faced with pressure and uncertainty, we chose courage over complacency and discipline over convenience.

As you read, I invite you to reflect on questions that define responsible decision-making:

1. How do we balance aspiration with capacity?

2. How do we maximize what we already have before chasing what we can't afford?

3. How do we preserve the systems that protect our health and well-being for the long term?

4. How do we help others understand—and accept—the necessity of difficult and sometimes unpopular decisions?

The Bison Principle offers a practical framework for professionals, a decision-making lens for appointed and elected officials, and a form of civic education for community members who care about the places they call home.

The message is simple but demanding.
Speak the truth.
Protect what matters most.
Confront what is hard.

CHAPTER 2

THE HEART OF THE MATTER

> "Society grows great when elders plant trees whose shade they know they shall never sit in."
>
> – Greek Proverb

Parks and recreation are one of the clearest expressions of what local government exists to do: strengthen health, foster connection, and improve quality of life. They are the part of the government that people see and touch most often. Someone may never attend a council meeting or read a budget document, but they'll notice whether parks feel safe, pools are open, restrooms are clean, and kids have something to do after school.

But the very visibility that makes parks and recreation beloved also makes them vulnerable when expectations change, and civic obligation erodes.

Our relationship with local government has shifted over the years. Instead of citizens with shared responsibility, we expect services as consumers. We view government as a vendor, not a partner. We see taxes as transactions, not investments. As this mindset grows, expectations rise while understanding wanes.

"I pay taxes, so I deserve everything I want" has become a common worldview. It assumes community systems exist to deliver personal satisfaction rather than mutual benefit. When people no longer feel part of a shared "us," their willingness to invest in their community declines.

If everyone demands more while resisting trade-offs, unsustainability becomes the inevitable outcome, and the systems we rely on eventually fail. That mindset distorts what local government actually is: a shared enterprise of care and an expression of belonging and investment in one another.

Parks & Recreation are Public Health

At their core, parks and recreation are a public health service. They are preventive medicine for the body, mind, and spirit—a health intervention often overlooked but actually hiding in plain sight. Every park bench and walking trail is an act of care. Every swim lesson, senior fitness class, or after-school program is intended as a commitment to longevity, connection, and hope.

Yet unlike hospitals or clinics, parks and recreation don't always get recognized for what they prevent. We notice when a playground opens, not when it keeps children active and healthy. We celebrate a new trail but overlook how it keeps isolation and depression at bay. Parks and recreation quietly sustain public health, often without awareness.

Why This Work Matters

After 35 years serving the public parks and recreation profession as a practitioner, educator, and consultant, I have seen both the brilliance and the burden of this work.

I have witnessed the joy of a child discovering nature for the first time and the heartbreak of a once-vibrant facility now shuttered for lack of funds.

I have sat in budget meetings where good people justified unsustainable decisions because it was politically easier than saying no. And I have watched communities lose the very services that once gave them life, not because they stopped caring, but because they simply didn't count all of the costs.

I still remember my early days as a recreation coordinator when I asked our finance director for a modest budget increase to buy additional supplies that had not been planned. His reply: *"Sure. Don't worry about the money."*

He meant it kindly. It troubled me. Years later, during the Great Recession, I watched as county, city, town, and special district budgets were cut to the bone, and once untouchable services began to vanish. The words *"don't worry about the money"* echoed louder than ever and haunt me to this day because the truth is, the money always matters.

That moment, and countless others like it, cemented my conviction: if we don't understand and respect the math behind the money, we can't honor the mission it is meant to support.

The Hard Truth About "Essential"

At its core, parks and recreation exist to steward public spaces and experiences that support community well-being. That purpose is broad by design, but it is not unlimited. Not everything in parks and recreation is essential. We have pursued good intentions with unclear priorities, attempting to serve every interest, thereby diluting impact.

Somewhere along the way, we began equating *activity* with *impact* and *variety* with *value*. We added facilities and expanded offerings because saying yes felt like progress and saying no meant sitting with discomfort and tension. Yet every "yes" carries a cost. Every new service diverts time, space, and dollars from something else—often services that serve the broader community rather than individual interests. The uncomfortable truth is that when everything is treated as essential, nothing truly is.

"We just need more money" misses the point; it's also about responsibility. Without discipline, extra funds feed unsustainable habits. We must clarify what is valuable versus what is merely popular, and what strengthens health versus what merely fills a schedule.

Financial discipline requires acknowledging that prioritization is not abandonment; it's leadership. It's the courage to say: *"We can't do everything, but what we do will matter."*

In public service, success should be measured by whether our choices make communities healthier, stronger, and more resilient over time, with a focus on lasting impact.

What We've Forgotten

Behind every ribbon-cutting—every new park, facility, or service—is a financial decision.

With every new recreation center and every "free" event comes a trade-off, one that will determine whether that service can be sustained or becomes a liability.

In the race to grow, we've lost balance. Financial reality too often takes a back seat to expansion and the allure of "more." It's not that growth is bad; it's that unchecked growth without a financial plan leads to fragile systems, community disappointment, and strain.

Financial discipline isn't about austerity,
it's about respect.

Respect for the taxpayer.
Respect for the professionals doing the work.
And respect for the next generation, who will
inherit whatever we build or neglect today.

CHAPTER 3
OUR QUALITY OF LIFE

> "When people love their cities, they invest more of themselves in them."
>
> – Peter Kageyama

The promise of parks and recreation has always been about more than green space, playgrounds, or programs. It has been about what those things make possible—health, safety, connection, and the pride of living somewhere that feels cared for and that people care about. Essentially, the things that help define the character of the places we live and our shared quality of life.

In local government, the phrase *quality of life* is often repeated in plans, reports, speeches, and mission statements, but it is rarely defined and remains one of the least examined ideas in public service. The irony is that while *quality of life* is the reason most people care about their city, it's also the measure most absent from how cities evaluate themselves.

Measuring What Matters

Acres of parkland can be counted, attendance calculated, and tax revenue measured, but those numbers alone do not reveal what people experience. A city can be statistically prosperous and emotionally impoverished at the same time. What distinguishes one place from another is not found in a single measure, but in its quality of life—the invisible fabric of relationships and pride that no spreadsheet can fully capture.

The truth is simple but often ignored: people don't fall in love with cities because of their efficiency. They fall in love because of how those cities make them feel.

Quality of life lives in the moments between metrics. The sound of children playing in a park, the safety of walking home at dusk, the way the community shows up for a neighbor in need. It is found in beauty, connection, and a sense of shared dignity. When those things are absent, no amount of infrastructure or branding can fill the void.

Acknowledging the limits of measurement does not remove responsibility—it sharpens it. When outcomes resist simple quantification, leaders must rely on a broader form of evidence: patterns of use, consistency of care, who feels welcome, and who quietly opts out. These signals may not fit neatly into a dashboard, but they are no less real, and they demand sound judgment, disciplined decision-making, and accountability.

Parks and recreation sit squarely in this space. They touch the emotional infrastructure of a community. They are where the city becomes visible to its people and where government ceases to be an abstraction and becomes a lived experience.

Social Fabric

In the early days of the American parks and recreation movement, the work was rooted in a clear and holistic understanding of human well-being. Parks were not built merely for leisure or diversion, but as tools for public health, social reform, and civic beauty. Reformers, planners, and early park leaders understood that access to green space, fresh air, play, and shared public life was essential to healthy cities. Parks were designed to counteract the physical and social toll of industrialization and to humanize daily life in rapidly growing urban environments.

These early systems were woven into the fabric of everyday living. Neighborhood parks, playgrounds, boulevards, and civic spaces were meant to be close to home, easy to access, and shared across social and economic lines. Their value was not measured primarily in attendance counts or revenue, but in healthier residents, stronger communities, and a more humane public realm.

Over time, that integrated ideal began to fracture. As local government expanded and professionalized, responsibilities splintered. Economic development interests pursued jobs and tax base. Tourism initiatives chased visitors and hotel nights. Parks and recreation narrowed its focus to the number of programs and facilities provided. Each function developed its own language, metrics, funding mechanisms, and governing bodies. What had once been a shared civic mission became a set of parallel efforts, often working at cross-purposes. The world changed, but many of our systems and foundational assumptions did not.

As Jeff Siegler, writer and researcher focused on the health of community systems and public places, and author of *Your City is Sick*, wrote, *"It's not about jobs and visitors anymore. It's about residents. It's about beauty, emotion, and attachment."* That shift is not sentimental, it's strategic. Cities thrive when their people love where they live. When residents feel safe, proud, and connected, they invest more of themselves in their community. They volunteer, support local businesses, advocate for their parks, and defend what they value. Love becomes an economic force, not a distraction from it.

Parks and recreation professionals have always understood this, often instinctively. They build places that make people proud. They host events that turn strangers into neighbors. They design experiences meant to foster connections. The challenge before the profession is not to rediscover this purpose, but to reclaim it—intentionally, systemically, and in ways that align with fiscal realities.

The Power of Beauty and Belonging

Beauty is not a luxury. It is a civic necessity. It is found not only in natural landscapes, but in clean and cared-for spaces, in thoughtful design, in safe and welcoming places, and in the quiet order of public environments that function as intended. Beauty signals that a place is valued—and that people matter.

When a park is well-tended, when a trail feels safe and intuitive to use, when a downtown is walkable, coherent, and inviting, people internalize those cues. They believe their city cares.

Peter Kageyama, community strategist and author of *For the Love of Cities* book series, calls this "emotional infrastructure", the invisible network of feelings that connects people to a place and creates a sense of belonging. When it's strong, a city can endure hardship, disagreement, even scarcity. When it's weak, every inconvenience feels like a betrayal.

Parks and recreation are the scaffolding of a community's emotional infrastructure—where a community learns to love itself through beauty, care, and shared use.

This connection between beauty and belonging lends greater meaning to financial decisions. It is not only about maintenance schedules and budgets; it's about making disciplined, long-term choices that honor people and place. When public resources are invested with care and intention, communities receive a clear signal: you matter, and this place is worth sustaining.

When cities neglect beauty, we see it in crumbling facilities, overgrown medians, and tired playgrounds. Deferred maintenance becomes a symbol of disrespect for the community.

Value

People routinely invest more, financially and emotionally, in things they value. A meal at a favorite restaurant, a concert ticket, a brand-name coffee, or a car that reflects identity all cost more than their basic alternatives. In each case, people are not paying simply for function; they are investing in meaning, connection, and pride. The same dynamic applies to the services cities provide.

That is why the work of parks and recreation matters so deeply. It gives form to the intangible by translating emotion into place and place into value. The trail that connects neighborhoods, the playground shaded by trees, the concert on the lawn—these are not luxuries. They are a civic return on investment.

Quality of life cannot be bought cheaply or delivered efficiently. It is cultivated slowly, through trust, design, and intention. It asks cities to measure success not only in dollars saved or projects completed but in people's willingness to stay, participate, and believe in its possibility.

Aspiration and Arithmetic

The paradox, of course, is that while quality of life

has never mattered more, it has never been harder to sustain. The ideals that make a city lovable are often the first to suffer when budgets tighten. Yet this is where courage meets fiscal stewardship.

If a city's true wealth lies in how it makes people feel, then maintaining that emotional infrastructure is not optional; it is essential. The moments when communities must choose whether to retreat from what is hard or to hold steady around what truly sustains them matter most.

Parks and recreation stand at the intersection of aspiration and arithmetic. Math alone cannot hold a community together, and meaning alone cannot pay its bills. The work ahead is to reconcile the two and ensure that what makes a place worth living and loving is not compromised by short-sightedness and the fascination of wanting more.

The New Era of Responsibility

In this era, parks and recreation organizations are not merely service providers. They must carry the responsibility of managing resources responsibly, connecting residents to their city and to each other, building social capital, and thoughtfully managing services and maintaining assets. They must embrace the full weight of that responsibility.

This isn't about replacing old institutions but about transforming them. As the civic landscape shifts, the mission must evolve from consumption to connection, from amusement to attachment and belonging. The measure of a thriving community will not be how many visitors it attracts, but how deeply its residents care about it.

The real work of quality-of-life professionals, especially those in parks and recreation, is to make that care visible. To help people fall in love with where they live, and to sustain that love through thoughtful design and long-term care.

CHAPTER 4
A PARADOX

> "It is not enough to have a good mind; the main thing is to use it well."
>
> – René Descartes

Across the United States, local governments confront a growing and uncomfortable truth: the math no longer works. Decades of expansion, deferred maintenance, and structural imbalance have brought many communities to the edge of a fiscal cliff. Costs are rising faster than revenues, infrastructure is aging faster than it can be replaced, and the public's appetite for amenities shows no sign of slowing down. What many communities are experiencing is not a sudden crisis, but the long-delayed arrival of consequences.

At the center of this crisis sits a service area that, for generations, has defined what it means to live well in a community: parks and recreation. Once regarded as proud symbols of civic health and community identity, park and recreation systems have become among the first casualties of fiscal stress. This paradox—that the very services credited with a community's quality of life are often treated as expendable—reveals much about how local governments have lost their fiscal footing.

From Expansion to Erosion

The origins of today's fiscal crises reach back decades. Communities grew, often rapidly, and built generously. Parks, trails, recreation centers, sports complexes, aquatic facilities, and cultural venues reflected optimism, ambition, and the physical expression of a community's aspirations.

Much of this ethos has noble beginnings. Public works like the Civilian Conservation Corps and other Depression-era investments were designed to strengthen both people and places, but their long-term care was rarely part of the story.

Few asked the harder question: *Can we sustain what we build?*

The focus was on ribbon cuttings, not replacement costs. The logic of "build now, pay later" became a cultural norm in local government, quietly creating long-term financial liabilities that outlived the administrations that approved them.

The result: expansive systems with limited means to maintain them. Deferred maintenance grew, infrastructure aged, and costs have become too large to ignore.

Misaligned Perceptions of Value

Parks and recreation are often described as "nice to have," essential in spirit but optional in budget. In times of fiscal stress, they become the easy target. Unlike police or fire protection, their absence doesn't immediately threaten safety. Yet the benefits—improved physical and mental health, economic resilience, environmental protection, and social connection are quieter, cumulative, and easier to ignore.

This misalignment shows up not only in budgeting but in how communities think about growth. Parks and recreation are frequently highlighted to attract new residents, developers, and employers. Trails, open space, and recreation amenities are marketed as signals of quality, livability, and competitive advantage. They help sell neighborhoods and recruit talent.

Attraction, however, carries a different incentive structure than long-term care. What draws people and investment is often treated as complete once it is built, even though its value depends on continued care and capacity. When that distinction is lost, parks and recreation shift from long-term systems to short-term selling points.

This disconnect between what residents value and what decision-makers fund is a central flaw in how communities define essential services. The irony is that while parks and recreation contribute to the social fabric, civic pride, and the livability of a community, they are consistently the first to be sacrificed when financial responsibility is absent.

Short Termism

Local government finance systems were designed for a different economy. Heavy reliance on property and sales taxes leaves communities vulnerable to economic swings and changing consumption patterns. At the same time, state and federal support has declined, while the costs of labor, healthcare, energy, risk management, and capital renewal continue to escalate.

The result is a widening gap between what communities promise and what they can afford.

For many, fiscal cliffs are not sudden events but slow-moving consequences of structural imbalance, deferred decisions, and unrealistic expectations.

Few elected officials are rewarded for restraint. The politics of saying "no" are far more punishing than the politics of "yes." As a result, difficult but necessary choices are often deferred. Facilities remain open despite declining use, programs persist without evaluation, and resources are spread thin across systems.

This is not mismanagement so much as it is misalignment. Communities aspire to provide abundance without acknowledging limits and hesitate to engage in conversations about what should be maintained, what can be reduced, and what may need to end. Without a shared language around costs, trade-offs, and limits, decisions become reactive rather than strategic.

The desire to serve everyone has morphed into sustained pressure to provide everything. Spreading scarce resources too thin only guarantees that no one is well-served in the long run.

The Erosion of the Social Contract

Underlying all of this is a quiet shift in the

public's relationship with its government. Citizens increasingly see themselves as customers rather than as co-stewards. Expectations are high, patience is low, and the understanding that public services require shared responsibility has diminished.

The social contract—the implicit agreement between citizens and their government to balance wants with means—has weakened. When people expect everything but resist paying, when elected officials promise more but cannot pay the bills, trust erodes and cynicism grows.

To move forward, communities must rediscover how to align aspirations with capacity—not as a constraint, but as a governing discipline. Fiscal stewardship is not about cutting; it's about caring for what exists. It's about aligning aspirations with capacity and re-establishing trust that public resources are being managed wisely and transparently.

Financial sustainability is the end game; stewardship is the means. It is the daily practice of responsibility, humility, and long-range thinking. In the context of parks and recreation, it means designing systems that are financially durable and operationally sound.

If local government carries the responsibility for community well-being, then parks and recreation are its conscience and reminder that prosperity without prudence is short-lived. Fiscal cliffs are not inevitable; they are the predictable outcome of choices made without accountability. The challenge ahead is not merely to survive the crisis, but to redefine success itself: to measure progress not by growth, but by sustainability—not by more, but by enough.

Quality of life is not measured by how much we build, but by how responsibly we care for and sustain the places that enable health and our collective well-being.

Conditions for Fiscal Stewardship

Communities cannot achieve what they do not first practice. Financial sustainability is never accidental. It is the byproduct of culture, structure, and disciplined decision-making. Stewardship emerges only when certain conditions are present and protected. These are the preconditions that enable systems to remain upright as pressure intensifies.

1. Shared Language & Meaning

Without shared vocabulary and meaning, informed and disciplined decision-making collapses. Terms such as fiscal stewardship, financial sustainability, partnerships, and cost recovery are often used inconsistently and abstractly, frequently leading to confusion and distrust. Shared language and meaning are the first acts of alignment because they help unify and create greater understanding.

2. Cultural Readiness

Mature systems acknowledge limits. Acknowledging limits early is an act of strength, while denying them simply delays the reckoning. Fiscal stewardship requires a culture that treats trade-offs not as loss but as discipline in service to endurance. Mature systems ask: *"What will we stop doing to protect what matters most?"* and *"What can we truly afford to sustain?"* Avoiding trade-offs produces fragility; practicing them produces resilience.

3. Truth Before Trust

No community can act responsibly without honest information. Data cannot be curated for persuasion or convenience. Trustworthy data means there is a clear understanding of long-term obligations and transparency regarding costs, illuminating the why behind decision-making.

4. Alignment Between Vision, Capacity, and Resources

Vision without capacity is negligence disguised as ambition. Communities routinely adopt plans, services, and facilities that the system cannot support. Durable financial decision-making demands alignment between:

- Vision and what we aspire to do
- Capacity and what we have the means to sustain
- Resources and what we can responsibly invest in and recover

5. Equity with Endurance

Equity is not about offering more. It is about providing what matters most to the common good and investing where it strengthens the whole. Unfunded equity is performative; sustainable equity is accountable. Fiscal stewardship recognizes that ensuring access requires durability and that every dollar has an opportunity cost. Without a model of endurance, funding collapses and inequity results over time.

6. Policy as the Mechanism of Stewardship

Policy enforces and converts conviction into operating reality. Fiscal stewardship fails when it depends on election cycles; it endures when embedded in systems that outlast leadership and personality changes. Durable governance codifies how trade-offs are made and shields decisions from political volatility.

7. Leadership as Enforcer

Stewardship rises or falls on leadership courageous enough to tell the truth and competent enough to navigate it. Leaders:

- Tell the truth before they sell a plan
- Absorb pressure instead of transferring it to someone else
- Choose durability over popularity

Courage without competence is reckless; competence without courage is irrelevant. Enduring stewardship requires both.

When these conditions exist—shared language and meaning, system maturity, transparency, alignment, equity, and courageous leadership—sustainability ceases to be an abstract goal. It becomes an organic outcome of the culture itself. In the end, fiscal stewardship becomes not just a means to an end, but a mindset and the highest form of service. It's a promise that what we inherit will be preserved and improved for those who follow.

CHAPTER 5
ROOTS & REFLECTIONS

> "History is important. More than any other topic, it is about us. Whether one deems our present society wondrous or awful or both, history reveals how we got to this point."
>
> – James W. Loewen

The history of parks and recreation is not just a story of government; it's the story of how communities have chosen to invest in their collective well-being.

Public parks and recreation were deliberate creations. They were born of a collective belief that shared spaces and services could improve lives, strengthen social fabric, and serve the common good. From the beginning, every decision, whether made in council chambers, at the ballot box, or in the court of public opinion, was influenced by the voices, priorities, and expectations of community members.

To look forward responsibly, we must first look back at history not as nostalgia or context, but as a revelation of our collective choices. Understanding how and why parks and recreation came to be illuminates not only the values of yesterday but also the role of everyday citizens in shaping priorities and outcomes. And it challenges us to recognize that we, too, bear responsibility. That today's debates, investments, and trade-offs are the history our communities inherit.

The Story Begins Long Ago

Long before parks and recreation systems emerged, societies grappled with how people spent time beyond work and survival.

In ancient Greece, leisure was education. In medieval Europe, it became a moral concern. The Renaissance reclaimed it as art and meaning. Each era carried forward ideas about how people should live, rest, and relate to one another.

When those ideas reached America, they were reshaped by necessity and hypocrisy. Early colonists outlawed idleness, tying morality to labor. Later, prosperity blossomed—inextricably tied to systems of exploitation and inequity. Slavery financed the luxury of leisure for some, while others were denied both freedom and rest.

Out of those contradictions grew a new vision: that parks could be for everyone and that open space could nurture the body and a sense of belonging.

As American cities grew in the nineteenth century, parks emerged as a response to industrialization, overcrowding, and public health concerns. Leaders like Frederick Law Olmsted advanced the idea that access to nature was not a luxury, but a civic necessity—something that could restore the body, calm the mind, and strengthen social bonds in rapidly changing urban environments.

Over time, that vision expanded. Playgrounds and recreation programs took shape alongside conservation efforts that protected large landscapes for public use. During the twentieth century, governments invested heavily in parks and recreation as essential infrastructure—building trails, facilities, and community spaces that reflected both optimism and a growing belief that public space mattered. As the field matured, it became more professionalized, increasingly focused on equity, health, sustainability, and access.

1850s–1890s - The Urban Parks Movement

- Frederick Law Olmsted leads push for naturalistic public parks
- Central Park (NYC) opened in 1857
- Parks are seen as a remedy to urban industrialization and crowding

1880s–1900s - Playgrounds & Early Recreation

- Boston Sand Gardens founded (~1885) – first supervised playground
- Growth of YMCA and school gymnasiums
- Emphasis on play, volunteerism, and child development

1872–1920s - Public Access & Conservation Movement *(overlapping era)*

- Yellowstone becomes the first national park (1872)
- Expansion of State and National Parks
- Parks positioned as tools for equity and national identity

1930s–1960s - Government Investment & Infrastructure

- New Deal programs (Civilian Conservation Corps (CCC), Works Progress Administration (WPA)) built parks and trails
- WWII era shifts focus to community well-being
- Post-war economic boom expands public demand for recreation

1970s–Today - Professionalization & Purpose Redefined

- Creation of academic and professional standards for the park and recreation profession
- Focus on equity, health, sustainability, and access
- Parks and recreation are seen as a platform for human rights and community resilience

While the foundation of parks and recreation was built on public investment and civic ideals, the closing decades of the 20th century marked an inflection point, one that questioned the role of government and redefined the social and financial contract between local government and taxpayers.

By the late 1970s, economic pressures and political shifts ushered in a new era of scrutiny and financial constraint. For much of the twentieth century, parks and recreation systems had been funded primarily as public goods, with general tax revenues serving as the financial foundation and fees playing a secondary role. Proposition 13, the 1978 California constitutional amendment that limited property taxes and required two-thirds voter approval for local tax increases, became a national symbol of taxpayer revolt. Its effects rippled far beyond California, signaling a shift toward limiting government revenue and increasing public resistance to taxation.

While elements of this tax-limitation philosophy were later debated and adjusted, its influence endured and spread, shaping measures such as Colorado's Taxpayer Bill of Rights (TABOR) and similar tax-limitation policies in other states. Parks and recreation systems, still largely supported by taxes, were increasingly expected to supplement public funding with alternative revenue sources as fiscal constraints tightened.

Original Intent & Mission Creep

The consequences of this fiscal shift were not only financial but philosophical. With fewer guaranteed dollars, organizations sought to prove their value by expanding services in response to every demand, however niche or fleeting. In doing so, many drifted from their original mission of promoting health, equitable access, and conservation. This widening of scope, often called *mission creep*, stretched resources thin and reshaped the identity of public parks and recreation.

While well-intentioned, this pattern created a mismatch between expectations and capacity. Communities came to expect more, even as tax support eroded, leaving professionals and officials with the burden of sustaining systems that had grown beyond their means. What began as a responsiveness to public demand evolved into a structural imbalance and a fragility that persists today.

PART II: FORMATION

FACING STORMS

When bison sense a storm, they turn toward it. Not as individuals, but as a group aligned by shared direction and responsibility. Their formation determines whether disruption scatters them or carries them through.

Public institutions are formed in much the same way. In this context, fiscal stewardship is not a slogan but a discipline shaped by language, norms, and civic expectations, reflected in how public resources are described and what can realistically be sustained.

Facing storms requires courage, shared principles, and a willingness to move beyond storytelling toward responsibility. It means recognizing that formation—how people organize, make decisions, and hold one another accountable—matters before a crisis arrives.

Formation is shaped over time by what is rewarded, tolerated, and ignored until it becomes evident in culture, behavior, and the choices that define an organization.

CHAPTER 6

PRINCIPLES, GRIT, AND RESOLVE

> "In times of uncertainty, the most courageous leaders are those who resist easy answers, confront uncomfortable truths, and hold steady when others retreat."
>
> – Anonymous

I spent much of my early years on the softball field—playing, competing, and learning the demands of teamwork and responsibility. That commitment carried through high school and college, and eventually into coaching. As a coach, I immersed myself in leadership studies, reading books such as *The Art of War* by Sun Tzu. I was determined to understand what it meant to lead—not just manage a team but inspire one. At the time, I thought leadership was about strategy, motivation, and drive.

What I did not yet realize was that leadership is something more demanding. It requires the courage to challenge convention, ask hard questions, engage in difficult conversations, and make unpopular decisions.

Over time, and across many communities, that lesson has only deepened—and sharpened.

The Heart of Leadership: Courage

Courage is what separates leadership from management. It is what allows people to move systems forward rather than merely maintain them. Leading often means standing alone, absorbing resistance, and pushing through discomfort when retreat would be easier.

History reminds us of this. The individuals who have shaped our society and institutions for the better rarely set out to be admired. They acted because their values left them no alternative. Their courage changed systems, not just moments—exactly the kind of leadership public institutions require.

Courageous leaders are guided by a clear "true north". Their core values hold firm in the face of adversity and criticism. They do not seek approval or popularity; they understand that leadership often means standing up for what is right, especially when doing so is difficult.

Courage cannot be taught in a classroom. It is earned through experience, by stepping into discomfort, taking calculated risks, and standing firm in the face of resistance. Sometimes courage is loud and costly. More often, it is quieter and appears when few are watching: the lone voice in a conference room naming an unfunded obligation no one else wants to acknowledge, a leader who recommends delaying a popular project because the numbers don't add up, or a single honest line in a report that says what others are unwilling to write. These moments rarely earn applause, yet they shape the outcomes communities ultimately live with.

The Art and Practice of Leadership

In the summer of 2013, I found myself walking across Harvard's historic brick paths in Cambridge, Massachusetts, toward a program called *The Art and Practice of Leadership*. I didn't know it then, but I was stepping into one of the most defining experiences of my life.

Our class included 67 people from around the world—most of us consultants and educators, with just 13 from the United States. I was the lone representative who worked with local government, a reality that made me feel both exposed and strangely determined. I remember scanning the room and realizing immediately: this wasn't going to be a place where titles or résumés mattered. This was a place built for discomfort, discovery, and truth-telling.

What made the experience transformative wasn't what I learned about leadership, but what I learned about myself. The program didn't offer answers. Instead, it pressed me—hard—against my own assumptions. It made me sit with patterns I had long ignored, limits I didn't realize I had been dragging behind me, and stories about leadership that no longer served me. It demanded a kind of honesty that felt, at times, like standing in front of a mirror I couldn't look away from.

It was uncomfortable. It was liberating. And it fundamentally changed how I understand the work of leadership.

On the first day of the program, our lead instructor asked each of us to name our Achilles heel—the thing that keeps us from saying what needs to be said or doing what needs to be done. I was called on first (out of 67 people—my lucky day!). Without much hesitation, I admitted, "I am too concerned about what people think of me." One by one, the others responded. After we finished, the instructor announced that the vast majority of us had given the same answer and, without softening the blow, delivered a line I will never forget: "If, after eight days in this program, your answer to that question is the same, you need to find another job."

It was a moment that cracked something open in me. The realization that so many of us—people who advise, coach, guide, and teach individuals and organizations—were constrained by the same fear was both sobering and freeing. It reminded me that leadership is about courage. It is about telling the truth when it is easier not to. And it is about growing past the very things that hold us back from doing the work that actually matters.

That experience also revealed something I had not previously considered: the essence of leadership is helping people confront what they would rather avoid. It is about holding steady when certainty is in question, accepting tension without rushing to resolve it, and guiding others through change that asks them to consider something that pushes them outside their comfort zone.

When the Answers Aren't Clear

Some challenges cannot be solved by expertise, authority, or technical skills. They persist precisely because they demand change—perhaps a change in habits, expectations, values, or identity. These are the moments that test leadership most.

When pressure mounts, the instinct is to restore order as quickly as possible. There is a tendency to reach for fixes that feel decisive because action feels safer than uncertainty. But not all problems need solutions. Some need reckoning.

There is a difference between challenges that can be fixed and challenges that must be faced. Fixable problems respond to expertise and authority. Harder challenges demand learning, loss, and changed behavior. Treating the latter like the former only delays the inevitable and deepens the damage.

I remember sitting before a city council years ago alongside a parks and recreation director in the Phoenix metro area, explaining why a high-profile project—a new sports complex—was financially unsustainable. The project had political momentum, enthusiasm from the youth sports community, and a ribbon-cutting already being imagined. But the math didn't work. Together, we presented the findings and a recommendation not to proceed—at least not without a sustainable funding plan.

The room went quiet. A councilmember leaned forward and asked, "So you're saying we shouldn't build what our residents want?" The director took a breath and answered, "I'm saying we can't afford not to be honest about it."

That kind of courage and leadership under pressure is what financial responsibility requires. Our communities should expect nothing less.

The First Through the Wall

One of my favorite phrases is, *"The first through the wall is always the bloodiest."* I often hear people ask, *"Do you know any organizations that have done this before?"* as if waiting for someone else to take the first step makes the path easier.

There is courage in being "the first". The first through the wall always takes the hit—the wind, the debris, the criticism. But they also create the opening. What follows is never easy, but it becomes possible. Running into resistance, like running into a storm, is not reckless. It is recognition that what threatens the system cannot be avoided; it can only be met.

It is easy to focus on the exciting aspects of public

service such as launching a new program, designing cutting-edge facilities, or exploring ways to deliver exceptional customer experiences. These things are valuable, but they do not require courage.

What requires courage? The tough, often unpopular yet necessary decisions that determine whether a system will be sustainable in the future.

Many government services are at a crossroads. Challenges like aging infrastructure, budget constraints, and increasing community needs and expectations cannot be solved with incremental tweaks. They require bold action.

Take infrastructure, for example. Across the country, maintenance backlogs have ballooned into the billions, largely due to years of prioritizing new development over long-term care.[1]

In many cases, public infrastructure is built by the private sector as part of development and then transferred to local governments and taxpayers to be maintained into perpetuity. In other cases, local

[1] At the time of writing, national and state-level analyses consistently estimate deferred maintenance and infrastructure backlogs for U.S. public assets—including roads, utilities, parks, and public facilities—in the hundreds of billions to trillions of dollars. Widely cited sources such as the American Society of Civil Engineers' Infrastructure Report Cards, state asset condition assessments, and local government capital improvement and facilities plans document how prioritizing new development over long-term care has shifted substantial lifecycle costs to taxpayers.

governments invest in roads, parks, utilities, and facilities to support or attract private development, often based on expectations of future growth, revenue, and economic returns.

In both cases, the upfront investment is visible and celebrated, while the long-term obligation is underestimated. Whether infrastructure is built by developers or funded through public financing, the result is the same: communities incur decades of maintenance, replacement, and operating costs that must be borne long after the initial development occurs.

Growth is exciting. But growth also breeds debt. And leadership means ensuring that an organization is not just thriving today but remains viable for generations.

Letting Go to Move Forward

Change is hard, not because people resist change itself, but because they resist loss. I've watched capable, committed employees struggle not with new expectations, but with what those expectations quietly take away—a familiar routine, a role they once mastered, or the confidence that came from knowing exactly how things worked.

Every organizational transformation requires people to give up something, whether it's a process, a tradition, or a belief. The discomfort we see during change isn't about misunderstanding; it's about mourning what is being left behind.

True leaders understand this. They don't dismiss resistance; they understand it. And they still move forward.

Before I became a local government consultant focused on financial and organizational strategy, I served as an administrator for a park and recreation department. During my tenure, the department experienced significant budget reductions, with additional cuts expected in the coming budget cycles. In that context, we recommended raising fees for an exclusive master swim program used primarily by adults of means, including a city councilmember and his friends. The program was heavily subsidized with taxpayer dollars that could have supported other services with far greater community impact.

The decision should have been operational, but our city manager, anxious about political backlash, required us to take it to the council. When the item came up, the councilmember in question became belligerent. We exchanged words at the dais, leaving the room tense and quiet. The next morning, I was called into the city manager's office and told in no uncertain terms to back off.

That conversation was supposed to humble me, but it did something else: it clarified my purpose. I realized then that speaking truth to power, even when the cost is personal, is a fundamental act of leadership. That experience was among the reasons I eventually left practice for consulting and a defining moment: I wanted to help others develop the courage to confront reality and act in the long-term interest of their communities.

The Body Politic

The phrase *Body Politic* dates back centuries and refers to a community as a single, living organism—citizens, institutions, and systems bound together by a shared fate. At its best, politics is meant to be a force for cooperation and collective care, providing the structure through which communities govern, thrive, and endure.

But the *Body Politic* weakens when power is used to serve narrow interests rather than the whole. In those moments, governance shifts and public decision-making becomes a form of political theater rather than civic responsibility.

This tension is not new. In 1513, a disgraced diplomat named Niccolò Machiavelli wrote *The Prince*, a blunt examination of how power is gained and preserved. His argument was unsettling but enduring: political success is often rewarded regardless of the methods used to achieve it. Results, he observed, frequently eclipse ethics in the public eye.

The echoes of Machiavelli remain visible today. Some elected officials are genuine champions of parks, recreation, and community well-being. Others operate with calculated precision—advancing personal legacy, catering to special interests, or pursuing short-term wins. When financial discipline is reduced to political maneuvering, the *Body Politic* suffers. When it is grounded in shared values and long-range responsibility, the system holds.

Leadership, at its best, is the discipline of not losing sight of the whole even when the noise, pressure, and incentives pull in another direction.

Political Decision-Making

Elected officials operate under constant and competing pressures from constituents demanding specific services, interest groups advocating for favored projects and protections, and fiscal realities that limit what can be promised and sustained.

Most enter public service with sincere intentions to serve their communities well. And many do. But the structure of political life creates powerful incentives that shape decision-making in ways that are rarely acknowledged out loud.

Re-election matters. Visibility matters. Public approval matters. Decisions are made not only in board rooms or council chambers, but with an eye toward the next election cycle, the next headline, the next public meeting, and the next organized group likely to show up and speak the loudest. These realities do not make elected officials unethical, but they do make governing more complicated than the public often assumes.

The tension emerges when short-term political survival conflicts with long-term stewardship. Projects that are visible, exciting, and popular are easier to champion than those that are responsible, restrained, or preventative. Saying "yes" often feels safer than saying "no," because "no" can carry real political cost.

This is where professional staff plays a critical, and often uncomfortable, role. Their responsibility is not to win elections, but to protect the long-term health and well-being of the system and community.

They are charged with presenting facts, evaluating impacts, and offering recommendations grounded in data, equity, and accountability, even when those recommendations complicate political narratives or threaten popularity.

Here is the hard truth many public employees eventually confront: appointed and elected officials are not obligated to follow professional advice, no matter how sound it may be. They can instead choose the path of least resistance, deferring difficult decisions, prioritizing short-term approval, or advancing projects that are popular but misaligned with long-term capacity—leaving staff to manage the consequences long after votes are cast.

Leadership in this environment is not about control; it is about endurance. It is about continuing to speak honestly when the outcome is uncertain, absorbing pressure rather than deflecting it, and resisting the temptation to soften reality for the sake of comfort. A single impassioned speaker, an organized interest group, or a looming election can quickly distort priorities. The test is whether leaders allow those forces to redefine the system—or whether they hold steady around what the community can actually sustain.

This is leadership under real conditions. Not idealized. Not theoretical. It is the discipline of weighing values alongside votes, math alongside growth, and long-term consequences alongside short-term rewards. It does not shield professionals from politics; it asks them to navigate it without surrendering fiscal stewardship.

Most people who choose public service, whether as staff or elected officials, are guided by ethics, commitment, and a genuine desire to do good. Yet even the most principled must operate within systems that can reward immediacy over endurance and approval over accountability. In that tension, leadership is proven by the willingness to keep pointing toward the storm when avoiding it would be easier.

Principles and Grit

The focus of any organization cannot be solely on shortcomings or potential missteps. Instead, it must be directed toward the principles of due diligence, long-term care, and a steadfast commitment to integrity. For those willing to take on the challenge, the wall to move through is rarely abstract. It is built on political pressure, public expectation, and the fear of being the one to name limits or say no. For those willing to go through that wall first, clarity, courage, and discipline must be their armor. Yes, the first through the wall tends to be the bloodiest, but it is also how real change begins. And no one needs to go at it alone.

That armor is strengthened through relationships. Seeking out others. Building connections with those who understand the cost of courage, the importance of principle-centered work, and are committed to something greater than comfort or popularity—mentors, allies, and advocates. Leadership in isolation is unsustainable; even the boldest amongst us need community. Sharing the weight doesn't make the work less complicated; it makes it more possible.

CHAPTER 7
MEANING AND PRACTICE

> "A common language is the most obvious binding element in any society."
>
> – Michael Howard

In my work, I have seen moments when the breakdown begins not with numbers, but with words. Before budgets fail or infrastructure deteriorates, meaning begins to slip. Familiar terms are used without examination. Assumptions go unchallenged. People believe they are aligned when they're not.

Few phrases reveal this more quickly than *cost recovery*. I have watched shoulders tense and conversations stall the moment the term enters the room. For some, it signals conflicts between profit-making and public service. For others, it feels like a quiet abandonment of purpose. The reaction is visceral—an immediate discomfort that shuts down dialogue before understanding has a chance to build.

Before any discussion about *cost recovery* can be productive, there must be a shared understanding of the cost of doing business—the real cost of providing services. Staffing, utilities, maintenance, administration, and long-term replacement all exist whether or not they are acknowledged. These costs do not disappear when they are ignored; they are simply absorbed elsewhere or deferred to the future.

Cost recovery is not the act of charging. It is the act of deciding intentionally and transparently what portion of known costs should be recovered from users, what portion should be supported by taxpayer resources, and why. It is not about profit. It's about proportion.

This pattern of disconnected meaning is not unique to the phrase *cost recovery*. It reflects a broader truth: when language breaks down, the ability to make responsible decisions does too.

These fractures rarely surface when resources feel abundant—when revenues appear stable, services expand, and daily operations are manageable. In those moments, language can remain loose because the consequences of misunderstanding are not visible or felt.

But when conditions tighten—when expectations

rise faster than revenue, when infrastructure ages, when trust becomes more fragile—those gaps widen. The questions that follow are no longer aspirational. They are immediate and uncomfortable.

What happens when there is limited public interest in or the ability to pay more?

What services can no longer be sustained at their current level?

And how long can growth be treated as a solution?

Questions like these require clarity about the meaning of what words like *essential*, *affordable*, or *equitable* actually commit an organization to in practice.

When Accountability Becomes Unclear

A councilmember once told me, with complete sincerity, "We rely heavily on *property taxes* to fund parks and recreation." The problem was that the community did not collect property taxes for parks and recreation. The system depended almost entirely on sales tax and tourism revenue, both highly sensitive to economic downturns.

The statement reflected no ill intent. It revealed a lack of understanding about where funding actually came from, who carried the risk when conditions changed, and what message was being sent.

On another project, staff urged our team not to recommend raising field rental fees for local youth sports organizations. “We need to keep our prices *affordable*,” someone said. “Parents will complain... loudly.” The conversation stalled—not because the data were unclear, but because the discomfort with perceived conflict over what *affordable* meant outweighed the willingness to set limits.

In moments like these, responsibility does not disappear. It becomes unclear, spread thin across good intentions, habits, and unspoken assumptions. Decisions default rather than being chosen, and language softens the reality of what is happening. Over time, trust erodes between what is said, what is understood, and what action is taken.

Public service rests on a promise: that those entrusted with shared resources will act with integrity and respect for the people they serve. Fiscal stewardship gives that promise structure and consequence.

Fiscal stewardship is the practice of matching resources with purpose and decisions with stated values. It combines financial discipline with human empathy and a long view of consequence. Language matters because fiscal stewardship depends on shared meaning. Without shared meaning, even well-intentioned decisions can strain systems and compromise the future they were meant to protect.

Words That Quietly Shape Decisions

In local government, certain terms recur in discussions of budgets, pricing, and public investment. They are often used interchangeably, assumed to be understood, and rarely examined. Each determines how burdens and benefits are distributed and what is protected when resources are limited.

Full cost represents the complete and ongoing expense of providing a service, including direct operations, administration, maintenance, and eventual replacement. It establishes the baseline against which pricing, subsidy, and investment decisions are made. Ignored, organizations make affordability claims without understanding how the unpaid balance will be covered over time and by whom.

Cost recovery is the intentional decision about the portion of a service's full cost to be recovered by users and other sources and the portion to be supported by taxpayer funds. It is not a revenue target or a profit mechanism; it is a proportionality decision grounded in known costs and public purpose. Misunderstood, it becomes either a political shield or a barrier to transparency.

Subsidy is a conscious decision to allocate taxpayer funds to offset the cost of a service for specific users or outcomes. A subsidy must be justified by a defined public benefit that exceeds the private benefit received. Left undefined, subsidies persist by default rather than by choice, obscuring who pays, who benefits, and whether the return warrants the investment.

Essential services are necessary to prevent harm, meet legal obligations, or protect core public functions. Not all valued services are essential, particularly when resources are constrained. Labeling a service as essential commits an organization to prioritizing it over others during periods of scarcity.

Affordability refers to whether the price of a service is set intentionally relative to its full cost and to the availability of subsidies. It is not synonymous with low price or universal access. When services are labeled affordable for users who have the ability to pay, public subsidies are consumed without advancing broader community benefits, limiting their availability for those with greater need or for services with higher public returns.

Ability to pay reflects the financial capacity of individuals or households to absorb fees or taxes without undue hardship. It is distinct from willingness to pay and must be assessed at the population level rather than through anecdotal evidence or the volume of complaints. Invoked selectively, the ability to pay becomes a proxy for pressure rather than a measure of need.

Equity refers to the intentional and proportional use of public resources to address unequal starting conditions or disparate impacts. It is not synonymous with equality or generalized notions of fairness. Equity requires that deviations from standard pricing or access be justified by a defined purpose and measured against the opportunity cost of using subsidies elsewhere.

Partnership refers to an arrangement in which cost, risk, and benefit are meaningfully shared among parties. When one party retains most of the benefit while the public assumes the majority of the cost or risk, the arrangement functions as a subsidy regardless of how it is labeled. Clear partnership agreements protect public resources from informal commitments or unintended consequences.

Shared understanding and disciplined use of these terms guide intentional decision-making and clarify responsibility for the use of taxpayer resources.

Clarity in Practice

In a small Colorado community, the city expanded its annual Halloween event and publicly reported achieving 51 percent cost recovery through sponsorships, fees, and partnerships, with the remaining costs covered by taxpayer dollars. That disclosure did something practical: it made cost recovery understandable. Residents were assisted in understanding the event's cost and the portion collectively funded by the community.

The value of that clarity was not the number itself. It was the visibility of the tradeoff. When costs, subsidies, and responsibilities are explicit, decisions can be debated on their merits rather than defended through assumption or emotion. The pressure remains, but it is grounded in shared facts rather than confusion.

Clarity, however, is only a starting point.

Understanding costs, benefits, and responsibility still leaves an essential question unanswered: *by what standard should those tradeoffs be judged?* When resources are limited and interests compete, how does a community decide what warrants collective support and what does not?

Those decisions are not purely financial. They are civic. They require a shared understanding of what public resources exist to protect and promote, not for individual advantage, but on behalf of the entire community. That standard is the common good.

CHAPTER 8
CIVICS FOR THE COMMON GOOD

> "Ask not what your country can do for you—ask what you can do for your country."
>
> – John F. Kennedy

The common good is one of the oldest ideas in democratic life and one of the least understood. It rests on a simple premise: a community functions best when people act not only for themselves but with regard for one another and when individual well-being and collective well-being are not competing aims but connected obligations.

When all of us thrive, the common good is strengthened. When some are left behind, the entire system weakens.

The common good is not achieved through belief alone; it is achieved through behavior. In a democracy, that behavior manifests in the routines of civic life: participating, weighing trade-offs, following the process, and supporting decisions made for the whole. Civics is the mechanism by which the common good becomes real and how shared responsibility moves from principle to action.

Influencing the Common Good

Few public services shape the common good as profoundly as parks and recreation. Unlike functions that serve a single sector, parks and recreation touch nearly every aspect of community life, providing places for children to play, older adults to stay active, neighbors to connect, and expressing the civic intention that access to nature and open space should be accessible to all.

To keep these services financially sustainable and equitably accessible, leaders must balance optimism with realism:

- Optimism that parks and recreation strengthen health, connection, and quality of life and therefore merit public investment.
- Realism that resources are finite, not every demand can be met, and sustainability requires understanding priorities and practicing restraint.

Local governments must commit to prioritizing the common good, not merely the demands of the loudest interests. That means shifting focus from what is popular to what is essential.

Principles for the Common Good

1. The common good must benefit the whole community, not select groups.

This means prioritizing services and investments that serve broad, diverse uses, such as neighborhood parks, trails, and basic recreation access, over amenities that primarily benefit a narrow or influential constituency.

2. Achieving it often requires compromise and self-restraint.

Serving the common good may require limiting exclusive use, capping the number of services offered, or declining expansion that strains staff and budgets. It asks individuals and groups to accept less-than-maximum benefits so that the system remains viable for everyone over the long term.

3. Privilege long-term stability over short-term approval.

> This occurs when elected or appointed officials resist pressure to defer maintenance, underprice services, or approve new facilities without identifying the funding required to operate and maintain services and assets over time.
>
> 4. Decisions must reflect a "we" perspective, not a "me" mindset.
>
> A "we" perspective asks how a decision affects access, affordability, and durability across the community, rather than whether it satisfies a single interest or a single moment in time.

No public entity can provide everything for everyone. The work is to discern what is essential from what is desirable. When spending reflects priorities rather than popularity, communities grow stronger, and trust deepens.

Over time, many of us—residents and even those working within public systems have drifted from seeing government as 'us' to treating it as 'them'. We have become customers instead of citizens—a consumerization of citizenship that erodes shared responsibility. Taxes are increasingly regarded as optional fees, paid only if a service is personally used or desired, rather than as shared contributions that sustain the whole. Civic participation is traded for complaint when engagement shifts from deliberation, learning, and shared problem-solving to dissatisfaction and protest.

When shared obligation weakens, the willingness to invest in shared systems collapses. If everyone demands more while resisting or ignoring limits, fiscal instability is predictable. This distorts the government's purpose: not a vending machine of services, but a collective enterprise of care.

The Pursuit of Prudence

Public decisions too often chase the loudest demand rather than the long view. A single organized user group advocating for expanded hours, exclusive access, or new amenities can command more attention than the less visible needs of maintaining trails, playgrounds, or aging facilities that serve the broader community every day. Perhaps the problem isn't that some argue for their expectations better; it's that communities have stopped asking the more complex, more important questions. Popularity has replaced prudence. The result is the same: policies that serve the few while jeopardizing the many.

This pattern is not merely philosophical; it shows

up daily in public systems. Communities expect well-maintained parks, safe facilities, and abundant programs, yet resist the revenues required to support them. At the same time, shared spaces are often treated as limitless—overbooked, overused, and under-maintained—until they no longer function as intended. Economics has long predicted these outcomes and names the failure modes clearly: either people assume others will carry the burden, or shared resources are used beyond their capacity.

The Free Rider Problem

Mancur Olson, a political economist who studied how groups succeed or fail at collective action, warned that public systems break down when too many people benefit without contributing. As Olson described, when people benefit from public goods without helping to sustain them, systems falter.

We see it daily: the neighbor who enjoys well-maintained trails, uses them regularly, and expects them to remain safe and accessible, yet votes against every park levy that funds their upkeep; the parent who expects high-quality youth programs from the parks and recreation department but protests modest fee increases needed to operate them. When too many do this, we don't just shortchange the system; we shortchange everyone who relies on it. The outcome is chronic underfunding and frustration that obscures accountability.

The Tragedy of the Commons

Garrett Hardin, an ecologist who wrote about shared environmental resources, described how systems collapse when individuals maximize their own gains from a common asset. Hardin warned that when individuals pursue narrow interests within a shared resource, the whole system suffers.

In local government, this appears when one group dominates a shared public asset. A community pool intended for lessons, open swimming, and family use is booked almost entirely for a single competitive team. Courts meant for casual, drop-in play are reserved night after night by the same leagues. A field once open for informal use becomes an assumed exclusive home for a single organization. Over time, access declines, conflict intensifies, and a public resource quietly stops serving the public.

If economics names the failure modes, civics supplies the habits and expectations that keep shared systems intact.

Civics: The Discipline of Shared Obligation

Civics is the discipline that makes self-government possible. It shows up in how we set priorities, respond to limits, handle disagreement, and whether we support decisions made for the whole, even when they do not benefit us personally.

A financially and socially sustainable system cannot be built by a government alone. It requires citizens who understand that equity is not everything for everyone; that revenue keeps systems open and safe; that maintenance protects access; and that nothing is free—someone pays. When those truths are understood, people shift from consumers to co-creators. They stop saying “the city should...” and begin asking, “how do we help?”

The common good does not collapse because people disagree—disagreement is normal in a free society. It collapses when we disengage, when we avoid hard truths, when we fail to listen, and when we do not explain what must be understood. Fiscal sustainability is defeated by silence, convenience, and short-term comfort.

Civic duty is not an abstract ethic; it is the price of living in a community that intends to endure pressure, scarcity, and change. To share benefits is to share upkeep. A society that expects the rewards of everyday life, things like safe parks, reliable infrastructure, and shared services without the work of maintaining them, is extracting without investing.

When some withdraw from responsibility while continuing to benefit, others shoulder more. That is inequity. The burden does not disappear; it shifts to those who now carry a heavier load.

Avoidance comes in all forms. Residents demand improvements while denying costs. Elected officials speak of "investment" while hiding liabilities. Professionals deliver more with less under a veil of pride rather than as a warning. These behaviors compound and avoidance becomes the culture.

Civic duty serves as an equalizer when shared rules, expectations, and contributions apply to everyone, not just those with time, money, or influence. It ensures that access to public systems is balanced by participation in their upkeep, and that no single group can dominate a shared resource simply because it is louder or better organized. Shared benefit without shared obligation is not democracy; it is dependency.

If we believe in the common good, we must behave as if our actions affect more than ourselves. If we hope to pass on functioning communities to future generations, we must act as though we understand that others will inherit the consequences of our choices.

If we expect public systems to remain reliable, commitment to their upkeep must be reliable.

The Politics of Pleasing

The temptation to say yes to everything is real. Requests such as extended facility hours, additional field time for a league, discounted fees for a popular program, a new amenity tied to a vocal constituency, or a “one-time” exception may feel harmless in isolation. Saying yes often buys short-term peace, preempts confrontation and complaints, and signals responsiveness.

Saying no is harder. It requires explaining limits, calling out trade-offs, and accepting frustration from people who care deeply but see only their interests. The difficulty is that popularity and capacity rarely align. Some of the most visible and passionately supported services are the hardest to sustain, whereas essential investments, such as staffing and repairs, are less visible and easier to shrug off to a later date. Governing by popularity carries a price: deferred maintenance, increasing inequity, eroded trust, and structural deficits that surface long after the celebration fades.

We have also sanitized our language. We say investment instead of obligation. Improvement instead of expense. We talk about benefits far more than burdens, and when the language of limits disappears, so does the public's ability to think in limited terms.

The path forward begins not with more listening, but with better listening—engaged, considerate, and compassionate. Engagement must move from demand to deliberation: from "What do you want?" to "What are you willing to prioritize, protect, postpone, or pay for?" Pair every aspiration with its implication. Teach the trade-offs, not just the talking points. Turn public meetings into classrooms.

Our collective obligation is to teach, design, and govern in ways that pull people back into shared responsibility so that what we build together can last. When residents understand the reality, they begin to see local government as a partner rather than an adversary.

CHAPTER 9
THE SOCIAL CONTRACT

> "We are not born for ourselves alone."
>
> – Cicero

A contract is not what most people imagine when applied to public life. Contracts are transactional—they end when both parties receive what they came for. But the work of governing a community never ends. The benefits of living in a stable, functioning society are ongoing rather than episodic. For that reason, what binds people to one another and to their institutions cannot be merely contractual. It must be a standing covenant of shared obligation.

A social contract is the standing agreement that we accept shared limits and shared commitments in exchange for shared stability and shared benefit. It is not codified like a statute, but it is no less binding. Laws grant authority, the social contract grants legitimacy. The government may still function when the social contract fails, but it cannot be expected to do good for society when it does.

What We Owe

Any community that intends to endure relies on its citizens, officials, and public professionals to fulfill specific duties.

Citizens owe participation beyond complaint, a willingness to share in costs, and respect for decisions made for the whole, even when those decisions are not personally beneficial.

Officials owe truth over popularity, stewardship over applause, and decisions aligned with long-term capacity rather than the loudest short-term demand.

Professionals owe competence, candor, and the courage to tell the truth about limits and the choices those limits force, even when honesty is uncomfortable.

These are the terms of self government.

When any party breaks faith—when citizens consume without contributing, when officials choose politics over prudence, when professionals fall silent, the load does not disappear. It shifts.

When a few benefit from public systems without contributing to sustaining them, others must carry more. When some opt out, others absorb the cost. The burden is then redistributed. And redistribution without consent is extraction.

This is why the social contract is not a theoretical abstraction. It is the only guardrail preventing public life from devolving into a contest of advantage.

Terms of the Social Contract

For decades, the social contract was assumed. People implicitly understood that public life required contribution and restraint. That assumption has eroded. We now inhabit a culture in which demands are explicit and duties are negotiable: where benefits are claimed and obligations are optional; and where rights are expected and responsibilities are forgotten.

Society can withstand disagreement. It cannot withstand unilateral withdrawal from duty. When the social contract is unspoken, it becomes unenforced. When unenforced, it is eventually ignored.

Communities do not achieve the common good by catering to individual preferences, as doing so shifts the focus from "us" to "me." They achieve it by binding themselves to expectations that outlast elections, budgets, and convenience. Without those expectations, public systems become unstable and advantage the few at the expense of everyone else.

If we want to pass on functioning schools, safe parks, working infrastructure, and institutions worthy of trust, we must act with the intention of handing them forward intact. That is the time horizon of a social contract: we act not only for ourselves but for those who will live with the consequences of our choices.

We have reached a point where the social contract can no longer remain implicit. What was once cultural must now be explicit. What was once assumed must now be articulated, not because the idea is new, but because the memory of it is fading.

If the common good is to endure, then the obligations that make it possible must be boldly reclaimed in the open, not implied, not hinted, not outsourced to "those people who understand," but stated, shared, and expected.

These governance and accountability shifts must define the next era of public leadership:

- from hoping people act as stewards to requiring that they do,
- from assuming responsibility to

structuring it,

- and from relying on culture to codifying covenant.

CHAPTER 10
A CULTURE SHIFT: FROM STORYTELLING TO STRUCTURE

> "Well done is better than well said."
>
> – Benjamin Franklin

For more than forty years, the field of parks and recreation believed that if the story was told well enough and if the case was made loudly, emotionally, and convincingly, the public and their elected officials would choose to fund it. The story of the work was framed around wellness, youth development, social cohesion, economic value, and community identity.

I entered the profession during the height of the *Benefits Are Endless* era, a period when the field focused heavily on articulating the social, health, and economic value of parks and recreation. The assumption was simple: if communities understood the benefits, sustained support would follow.

We were right about the benefits, but we were wrong about the mechanism that would carry through financial and political pressures.

We now pay the price of that assumption. Parks are widely loved and consistently underfunded. Recreation is among the first cuts when budgets tighten. The public agrees that the services matter and still resists paying for them. In other words, belief rose, but support for paying more did not.

We convinced people that parks and recreation improve quality of life, but we did not build the structures that make quality-of-life services financially durable. We built use without upkeep. We enabled expectations without obligation. We invited consumption without defining who bears the ongoing costs.

Taken together, these reflect a single gap: the absence of a durable financial structure embedded into how quality-of-life services are funded, managed, and governed. This is the gap the next era must close.

Stories can open people's eyes, but they cannot carry the weight of a system. Narrative without structure collapses the moment pressure arrives.

Bison don't survive storms because they believe in movement; they survive because their behavior is shaped by instinct, structure, and collective discipline. Systems are no different.

If we want parks and recreation to endure, the work must move beyond telling people why it matters to designing how it is sustained.

Correction by Design

We can see this lesson everywhere in public life, not just in parks and recreation. Systems fail when we treat agreement as a substitute for structure. People may believe in public schools, public safety, clean water, and safe streets, but belief alone doesn't keep teachers employed, roads repaired, or aquifers protected. Every public system that lasts is supported by rules, funding discipline, accountability, and responsible follow-through. Admiration has never been enough.

This is where civic life most often breaks down: we assume that if people care about something and there is sentiment attached, they will sustain it.

Narrative can open the door, but only a well-designed structure keeps the door from closing again when pressure arrives. Suppose we want the services that make a community livable to still exist in a generation. In that case, we cannot continue to operate as if appreciation were the same as maintenance, or as if applause were the same as commitment.

Belief explains why something matters. Behavior determines whether it survives.

The Benchmark Trap

Even as local government has embraced data and measurement, we often use them in ways that preserve the very habits we claim to outgrow. National standards and benchmarks, for example, are often held up as proof that an organization is "performing well." But benchmarking can be its own kind of storytelling—an appearance of discipline without the substance of understanding.

The hidden assumption behind benchmarking is that those we compare ourselves to are doing things right. In practice, benchmarks often reflect what is common rather than what is defensible. Yet many of the agencies used for peer benchmarking exercises struggle with deferred maintenance and structural deficits, and follow unsustainable subsidy patterns, such as arbitrary service pricing. When their numbers are used as a compass, the risk lies in aligning operational practices with dysfunction instead of excellence.

Benchmarking can be valuable, but only when it begins with context rather than imitation. It should clarify local truth, not validate national averages. Otherwise, we end up grading ourselves on a curve in a class that's already failing.

True stewardship requires the courage to ask: What does sustainability look like here, for us, in this place, in this moment, with the resources we have? That answer won't be found in anyone else's spreadsheet.

Temporary Relief is...Temporary

A similar illusion arises with funding. Some communities receive new or supplemental tax revenue through dedicated levies or other voter-approved measures and mistake that infusion for long-term fiscal health.

Levies are a specific type of voter-authorized tax, typically tied to a defined purpose or service, that provides revenue beyond a general fund. *Voter-approved measures* are a broader category of ballot actions that may authorize levies, bonds, taxes, or fees—often for specific uses and, in many cases, for a limited period of time.

While these funding tools can be transformative, they are conditional by design. They do not eliminate the need for disciplined financial management or long-term planning. When new revenue is treated as sufficient in itself without regular examination of costs, obligations, and service levels, risk quietly accumulates over time.

When new tax revenue becomes the expectation rather than the exception, systems begin to grow around it. New facilities are built, additional services are added, and obligations expand without any guarantee that funding will continue. Eventually, when the revenue plateaus or declines and expenses increase, the organization is left with commitments it cannot afford to keep.

Additional public dollars secured through levies or voter-approved measures should be treated as an embellishment, not a crutch. They can accelerate progress, but they cannot substitute for discipline. Fiscal stewardship demands that we build and operate only what we can sustain in perpetuity, with or without temporary boosts.

The goal is not simply to receive more funding, but to ensure that every dollar, new or old, strengthens the foundation rather than decorating the façade.

From Applause to Accountability

The next era must hinge on systems designed, governed, and financed in ways that compel responsible behavior, regardless of sentiment.

Budgets must reflect lifecycle costs—the full cost of operating, maintaining, and eventually replacing facilities and services. Policies must tie access to shared obligation. Elected officials must approve projects only when operations and maintenance paths are secured.

Fiscal stewardship must be treated as a precondition for decision-making regarding planning, investment, and service delivery.

This is the cultural shift required: designing something built to last.

PART III: RECKONING

THROUGH THE STORM

As storms intensify, comfort, delay, and illusion disappear. When bison run into the storm, there is no room for denial or drift, only forward motion grounded in instinct and resolve. Survival depends on recognizing reality and acting decisively, rather than waiting for conditions to improve on their own.

In local government, reckoning emerges through funding limits, mathematical realities, and policy choices that cannot be deferred. Growth reveals its true cost. Stability demands tradeoffs. Finite, shared resources force clarity about priorities, equity, and responsibility.

Reckoning is not failure.

It is the moment when assumptions are tested, and consequences become visible. When fiscal stewardship moves from aspiration to action, and policy becomes the means by which leadership decides what will be sustained, what must change, and what cannot continue.

CHAPTER 11
STABILITY VS GROWTH

> "Politicians should not have the pleasure of spending without the pain of taxation."
>
> – Frank Cavanaugh,
> Former Treasury official

With all the prosperity this nation has experienced, why do so many governments struggle to maintain what they already have? Why do parks, roads, and civic buildings—once points of pride—now strain for basic upkeep?

The uncomfortable truth is this: we built faster than we could sustain. We mistook expansion for success. The American landscape is filled with symbols of ambition—new subdivisions, recreation complexes, highways, and town centers—but the foundation underneath them is eroding. The crisis isn't just about infrastructure. It's about how we define progress.

For decades, our civic story has been told in square feet, lane miles, and ribbon cuttings. The story we must tell now is one of stability, not sprawl, and one of discipline, not spectacle. Growth without discipline is consumption on credit.

The Lesson: Bigger Isn't Better

In the decades following World War II, the prevailing American narrative was one of unquestioned growth. Suburbia, car-centric infrastructure, and endless expansion became shorthand for prosperity. More meant progress. Bigger meant better.

That story came with an unspoken cost. Communities added infrastructure and services at a breathtaking pace, but rarely budgeted for their maintenance or eventual replacement. Many of these decisions were made under the assumption that future economic growth and a steadily expanding tax base would cover those costs over time. What was celebrated as success was, in many cases, assumed liabilities disguised as civic achievement.

That assumption proved false. Economic growth did not materialize evenly. Household wealth trajectories flattened. Tax structures shifted in ways that constrained public resources. Yet the infrastructure remained. The belief that 'growth will pay for itself' collapsed once revenue no longer aligned with long-term obligations.

Today, the bills have come due. Across the country, governments face mounting backlogs, thinning maintenance budgets, and service cuts, not because of bad people, but because of bad math.

True strength isn't measured in what is built. It's measured in what can be sustained well over time. It's time for a new operating principle: *prioritize stability over growth, resilience over expansion, and value over volume.*

Case in Point: A National Pattern of Decay

In my work, I have seen this pattern play out repeatedly—in communities large and small, across regions, and at every level of government. The scale varies, but the math does not. We expanded far beyond our collective capacity to maintain.

It is important to say this plainly: many professionals managing these systems today did not create these conditions. Most inherited them. They are living with decisions made decades earlier, often under very different political, economic, and cultural expectations. But inheritance does not eliminate responsibility. It makes clarity more urgent.

Local – Milwaukee County Parks, Wisconsin

Milwaukee County Parks was once a hallmark of civic pride and professional excellence. In 1989, the system operated with a $37 million budget. Thirty years later, that figure was nearly unchanged in nominal terms despite inflation having cut its real value nearly in half.

The consequences were operational and human. Staff levels dropped from more than 1,000 to fewer than 500. Maintenance cycles stretched. Playgrounds aged without replacement. Trails cracked and closed. Facilities that once anchored neighborhoods became liabilities the system could no longer keep pace with.

The remaining staff worked longer hours, covered more territory, and made more difficult trade-offs, often deciding which problems could be deferred to another season. The maintenance backlog grew to more than $400 million. Milwaukee County Parks became a lesson in what happens when growth is celebrated, but care is postponed.[1]

State – Pennsylvania State Parks

[1] At the time of writing, Milwaukee County budgets have included incremental increases in operating support, the addition of maintenance positions, targeted capital reinvestment, and limited one-time infrastructure funding intended to stabilize the system and begin addressing deferred maintenance. While meaningful, these steps represent movements within a long-standing structural funding gap.

In 2024, Pennsylvania's 121 state parks drew more than 38 million visitors and generated roughly $1.5 billion in economic activity. For years, consistently high visitation reinforced the perception that the system was thriving. But growth accelerated wear. And wear demanded reinvestment.

The system accumulated an estimated $1 billion backlog of deferred maintenance.[2] Roads, dams, bridges, restrooms, water systems, and historic structures aged faster than available funding could address. Conditions eroded, often unnoticed, until failures became unavoidable.

Staff were asked to serve more visitors with limited resources, prioritizing immediate safety and access over long-term preservation. For visitors, the impacts appeared incrementally: closed amenities, aging facilities, and declining reliability. For staff, the work shifted from natural resource stewardship to triage.

Federal – The National Park Service

The National Park Service manages more than 400 units across 85 million acres, stewarding some of the most iconic landscapes and historic places in the

[2] According to a 2018 Pennsylvania Parks and Forests Foundation report, the parks and forests system had accumulated an estimated $1 billion backlog of deferred maintenance.

country. Over generations, visitation has increased steadily, reinforcing public expectations of access, care, and continuity.

Over the past decade, the system's maintenance backlog has grown to more than $23 billion, despite targeted investments. Much of the infrastructure—roads, water systems, visitor centers, employee housing, and utilities—was built in the mid-20th century and is now approaching the end of its useful life.

During this same period, deliberate federal decisions were made to reduce staffing levels, limit services, and close facilities. These decisions did not occur in isolation. They reflected choices about what would be protected, deferred, or compromised for future generations. As Theodore Roosevelt framed it when establishing the nation's conservation ethic, public lands are assets that must be passed forward *"increased, and not impaired, in value."* That standard clarifies what is at stake when reinvestment fails to keep pace with use.

The impacts extend beyond infrastructure. Fewer staff mean diminished interpretation, reduced resource protection, longer response times, and weakened institutional capacity. Facilities may remain open, but the ability to care for them erodes.

A Pattern: When Vision Blurs Reality

These dynamics are not abstract. They surface most clearly when communities attempt to plan their future without fully acknowledging the conditions they have inherited.

During a parks and recreation master planning effort for a city in California with a maintenance backlog in the hundreds of millions of dollars, this tension became explicit. During the review of the draft plan, the city manager expressed concern about publicly naming the backlog. He described the document as a visioning exercise and argued that existing maintenance liabilities should not constrain future aspirations.

He also noted that the city held approximately $12 million in reserves and was therefore "set up for success."

The moment was instructive. The underlying issue was the belief that vision could be separated from obligation—that aspiration could be discussed without confronting inherited conditions. Reserves do not erase backlogs. And visions untethered from existing realities do not guide; they obscure.

Across local, state, and federal systems, the pattern is consistent:

- Expansion outpacing reinvestment
- Maintenance and staffing treated as adjustable rather than essential
- Capacity erosion normalized over time
- Liabilities transferred forward to future generations

The people managing these systems today did not choose the starting conditions. But they are responsible for whether those conditions are named honestly and addressed deliberately. Until fiscal discipline receives the same attention and celebration as growth, communities will continue to pursue expansion while building systems they cannot sustain.

Digging Holes and Cutting Ribbons

When a new facility is built, everything feels easy: fresh paint, new systems, warranties intact. The first five years are the honeymoon. But eventually the shine fades, and costs appear—repainting, heating, ventilation, and air conditioning (HVAC) system replacement, irrigation repairs, and roof leaks.

By then, the elected officials who championed the project are often no longer in office. Liability remains.

Short-term wins are seductive. Groundbreakings and ribbon cuttings are exciting, visible, and politically rewarding. Maintenance budgets and renewal plans are invisible and therefore expendable. The result is a pattern of governing by optics, where short-term applause outweighs long-term responsibility.

We have built systems that celebrate creation and ignore preservation.

Imagine if we held ribbon-cutting ceremonies for repairs—oversized scissors and photo ops for roof replacements, trail resurfacing, and sewer line upgrades, cheering reinvestment and care with the same enthusiasm as new construction.

A longtime colleague works for a university in Texas that renovated a restroom and, rather than it becoming just another maintenance project, celebrated it in style. A press release, a ribbon cutting, poop emoji cookies, and small cups filled with lemonade to represent...well, you know.

That's the shift we need—maintenance not as mundane, but as an act of care and maybe even fun.

The Cost of Waiting

In Austin, Texas, decades of ambition have caught up with reality. A vast system of roads, parks, libraries, recreation centers, and more than 30 swimming pools built during a period of optimism and expansion. At the time, growth was synonymous with progress.

Half a century later, many pools are well beyond their useful life. Some leak thousands of gallons of water per day, wasting resources and increasing operating costs. Repairs were postponed year after year while new projects continued to be added. What began as a maintenance challenge became a fiscal, social, and environmental burden.

Deferred maintenance rarely collapses systems overnight. It erodes them gradually, until the scale of the problem exceeds the capacity to respond. Deferring maintenance is simply the choice to fix something later. But "later" never comes cheaply. It's how small cracks become structural failures or how temporary delays turn into permanent liabilities.

The late Dr. Albert Bartlett, a physicist at the University of Colorado, spent much of his career warning about the consequences of ignoring simple math. His famous lecture, *Arithmetic, Population, and Energy*, introduced generations of students and policymakers to what he called humanity's "greatest shortcoming"—our inability to understand the exponential function. He wasn't talking specifically about finance or infrastructure, but his warning applies to both. When small, unaddressed problems compound, they grow invisibly until they overwhelm the system meant to contain them.

That's the math of decline. A modest roof repair ignored today becomes a full replacement tomorrow, along with interior damage and downtime. Skipping maintenance of heating, ventilation, and air conditioning (HVAC) systems shortens the system's life by years. Deferred trail repairs multiply both cost and risk.

Small, consistent investments compound in the other direction, extending asset life, keeping costs predictable, and avoiding emergency replacements. Maintenance is not a cost center. It's compounded protection.

The Liability Paradox

In local government, every decision carries an obligation. New projects bring long-term costs for staffing, utilities, maintenance, and replacement. When we fail to account for those obligations up front, they become tomorrow's deficit.

Growth can be healthy, but only when it strengthens the system that supports it. Otherwise, expansion is disguised fragility. Governments often pursue growth to relieve financial pressure, only to deepen it. This is the liability paradox. Projects intended to signal success can become sources of future instability when financial discipline is absent.

Faithful fiscal stewardship flips that script by requiring sustainability to be tested—explicitly and rigorously—before commitments are made.

1. Lifecycle Costing

Every project should include the full cost of ownership—construction, operations, maintenance, and renewal. A $50 million facility can become a $150–200 million lifetime commitment.

2. Sustained Funding Rule

No new initiative without a dedicated, indexed funding source for ongoing costs.

3. Maintenance Before Expansion

Don't add new liabilities when the current system is under strain.

4. Generational Lens

Plan beyond the next election cycle. Consider the consequences of today's decision 30 years from now.

5. Transparent Math

Publish the data. Tie budgets to risk and condition. Let residents see where dollars go and why.

Fiscal stewardship lives behind the scenes in repair schedules, asset inventories, and preventive maintenance logs. Those don't make headlines, but they make systems last.

Rules alone aren't enough if our incentives point in the wrong direction.

Let's change what we celebrate.

- Hold ceremonies for reinvestment. Treat resurfaced trails, roof replacements, or ADA upgrades as civic milestones.
- Make maintenance visible. Use signage to connect improvements to funding sources and public benefit: "Your Tax Dollars at Work – Extending the Life of Community Assets."

- Report reality. Show the maintenance backlog publicly—not as shame, but as accountability. Progress bars, dashboards, and open data build trust.

When fiscal stewardship is treated as civic leadership, progress shifts from an economy of applause to an ethic of endurance. Every generation believes it's building for the future. But building alone isn't enough. Without discipline, growth becomes the very thing that weakens us.

True prosperity isn't in how much we build. It's in how long what we build serves well.

CHAPTER 12

FUNDING QUALITY OF LIFE

> "The first rule of sustainability is to align with natural forces, or at least not try to defy them."
>
> – Paul Hawken

Every public dollar tells a story. How it's raised, where it's spent, and what it produces reveal more about a community's values than any slogan or mission statement. Those stories shape public confidence and underpin the trust between communities and the institutions that serve them.

The Currency of Trust

When residents pay taxes or fees, they're not buying services; they're investing in their community. They trust that resources will be used wisely, responsibly, and with consideration for the future.

That trust is fragile. It can be strengthened through transparency or shattered by waste, arrogance, or neglect. Healthy communities understand that money isn't the problem, but that misunderstanding how money is used is. People tend to support public spending when they see evidence of care and competence. If these are absent, trust is fractured, and it becomes much harder to regain after it's lost.

Public services, including parks and recreation, are funded through a combination of mechanisms, each with distinct strengths, limitations, and implications.

1. Taxes: The Foundation of the Commons

Taxes are the original crowdfunding model. They are how we share responsibility for the places and systems that serve everyone.

- *Property taxes* tie directly to place, supporting the infrastructure that sustains home values and quality of life.
- *Sales taxes* capture broader spending by residents and visitors but can rise and fall as the economy fluctuates.
- *Other local taxes*, like income or utility taxes, spread costs more evenly but are less common.

Taxes are rarely popular, but they are essential. They

ensure that public safety, streets, parks, and clean, well-maintained areas don't depend on charity or chance. At the same time, tax-supported systems are shaped by political will and public consent, and remain vulnerable to shifts in priorities, competing demands, and governance failure. A tax-supported park system asserts that green space, safety, and play are rights of citizenship and commitments that must be actively upheld, not assumed.

2. Enterprise Funds and Use-Based Rates

Enterprise funds such as water, wastewater, stormwater, and solid waste are supported by rates tied to individual use rather than taxes. They are intended to cover the full cost of operating, maintaining, and replacing essential infrastructure. Similar funds can exist in parks and recreation, including golf courses, water parks, cemeteries, and marinas, where user revenues are expected to sustain both operations and assets.

3. Fees

Fees are charges paid by individuals for direct, personal use of a service or facility. Unlike taxes, which support shared public benefits, fees link use to contribution. In this way, fees translate personal use into personal responsibility.

When designed thoughtfully, fees can make systems fairer by ensuring that those who receive direct, individualized benefits contribute proportionally to the cost of providing them. The challenge lies in balance.

The goal is not to eliminate subsidies, but to align them, ensuring that public support flows toward services with broad community benefit, rather than toward activities that primarily serve individualized or specialized interests.

4. Grants

Grants can provide valuable resources to test ideas, address emerging needs, or enhance existing services. They are typically competitive, time-limited, and require ongoing compliance, reporting, and renewal. Even when awarded, grants are not guaranteed beyond their stated term and may be reduced, delayed, or discontinued as priorities, funding sources, or political conditions change.

For these reasons, grant funding is considered *soft money*, meaning it is temporary, conditional, and subject to renewal or withdrawal, and should not be relied upon for ongoing operations or long-term capital expansion without a clearly identified, sustainable funding plan. Using grant dollars to build new facilities or launch new services without secured operational and maintenance support can create unfunded liabilities and unmet community expectations once the grant period ends, if not sooner.

Grants should supplement existing capacity rather than create new obligations.

5. Sponsorships

Sponsorships are agreements in which private or nonprofit entities provide financial or in-kind support to enhance services or facilities, typically in exchange for defined recognition or association. Unlike charitable donations, sponsorships involve mutual benefit and clearly articulated terms.

When structured appropriately, sponsorships can increase community visibility, strengthen relationships, and generate resources without compromising public purpose. That structure matters. Sponsorships should be transparent, time-bound, and governed by clear standards to ensure they do not create preferential access, perceived influence, or misalignment with organizational values. When managed carefully, they can support public goals while maintaining public trust.

6. Donations

Donations can make a meaningful difference, particularly for amenities that inspire personal or community pride, such as playgrounds, trees, benches, or scholarships. They connect people emotionally to the places they care about and can strengthen the bond between residents and their public spaces.

Donations, however, are rarely simple. They require time, relationship-building, clear accountability, and ongoing communication. Donors often expect updates on how their contributions are used, and many gifts come with restrictions that limit where or how funds may be spent. While unrestricted donations offer flexibility, restricted gifts—those designated for specific purposes—can add complexity when they do not align with an organization's most pressing needs.

Like grants, donations should be treated as enhancements, not expectations. Philanthropy can enrich a system, but it cannot sustain one.

7. Partnerships

Partnerships, whether with nonprofits, businesses, or community organizations, can expand capacity and improve service delivery when designed with clear expectations and shared benefits. The rule of reciprocity governs effective partnerships: each party contributes and receives value that is equitable and measurable.

In practice, this might include shared-use agreements, co-programming, joint maintenance responsibilities, coordinated staffing, or resource sharing that extends reach or quality without imposing disproportionate costs on the public. When a local government provides more than it receives on behalf of residents and taxpayers, it ceases to be a partner and instead functions as a grantor. All partnerships, including sponsorships, should be structured to protect the public interest and demonstrate tangible community value.

8. Development and Impact Fees

Development and impact fees ensure that as communities grow, new development contributes its fair share to the infrastructure and amenities that make growth possible. These fees help offset the costs of additional parks, trails, streets, and utilities required to serve new residents or businesses.

When set appropriately, they promote fairness and ensure that existing taxpayers aren't left subsidizing the full cost of new growth. However, when fees are too low or inconsistently applied, they shift the financial burden to future budgets and erode long-term sustainability. Growth should pay for growth, not compromise the ability to care for what already exists.

9. Debt Financing

Debt is not inherently bad. When used prudently, it enables communities to build today for benefits that will be enjoyed for decades. In parks and recreation, debt is most commonly used to finance large, one-time capital investments such as land acquisition, major facility construction, or systemwide improvements that would be impractical to fund through annual operating budgets alone.

Primary debt vehicles used in parks and recreation are *general obligation bonds*, which are backed by the full faith and credit of taxpayers, and *revenue bonds*, which are repaid through dedicated income streams such as user fees, lease payments, or facility revenues. In both cases, borrowing represents a long-term financial commitment that extends well beyond the initial construction period.

Borrowing for capital investments can be appropriate when repayment plans are clear, funding sources are realistic, and future operations and maintenance costs are fully accounted for. The risk arises when debt becomes habitual—when "we'll figure out funding later" becomes practice. Borrowing for operations, short-lived amenities, or projects lacking broad community support creates the illusion of capacity while constraining future flexibility.

The Myth of "Finding the Money"

Oh, the times I have heard this refrain. "We'll find the money."

It sounds confident, even reassuring, but it's one of the most misleading phrases in public finance. The idea suggests that resources are misplaced rather than unavailable, and that creativity or persistence alone can overcome fiscal limits.

In practice, "finding the money" often means diverting funds from maintenance, deferring obligations, or borrowing against future budgets. It creates the illusion of solvency—the appearance that the organization can meet its obligations—while deepening structural imbalance. Each time the phrase is used to justify a new project or expense, it reinforces the false belief that local government can do more with less, indefinitely.

This mindset doesn't just distort decisions; it erodes trust. Residents hear the promise and assume a solution exists when, in reality, something else will be left undone. "Finding the money" is not a strategy; it's a story we tell ourselves to avoid hard choices.

Ironically, the riskiest financial decisions often occur in good times. When revenues are substantial, scrutiny fades, and expansion feels safe. But prosperity without control creates fragility.

Be Wary of Unicorns and Rainbows

Communities often plan for what they want rather than what they can fund. I encountered this dynamic when a town council member from a small, rural community in Colorado requested my perspective on a recently completed parks and recreation master plan.

The plan had been developed by an outside firm and followed a familiar process—community surveys, open houses, and a long list of identified "needs," including an indoor recreation center, ice rink, amphitheater, trails, and more. What was notably absent, however, was any meaningful fiscal analysis.

As we discussed the plan, it became clear that there was no defined path to pay for what had been proposed. The needs assessment functioned as a catalog of aspirations, disconnected from available resources, staffing capacity, or long-term operations. The resulting plan was unaffordable and unattainable.

When communities plan without financial grounding, they create cycles of frustration and illusion. Each new plan raises expectations, only to stall when funding realities set in. Over time, this erodes credibility and leaves both staff and residents wary of plans that promise much and deliver little.

Responsible planning must start with what a community can realistically build, operate, and maintain. It must be grounded in financial reality, with funding secured well before any commitments are made. A smaller, implementable plan builds more trust than an ambitious one that never sees the light of day.

CHAPTER 13
DOING MATH

> "How did you go bankrupt? Two ways. Gradually, then suddenly."
>
> – Ernest Hemingway, The Sun Also Rises

Math is a translator. It turns aspiration into accountability. It takes noble ideas like "enhancing quality of life" and translates them into questions that matter: How many staff hours will this take? How much will it cost each year? Will this decision limit our ability to maintain what we already have?

Too often, math is left out of the conversation until it's too late. Yet it belongs at the table from the start. Math is not a constraint on vision; it's what protects vision from collapse. It's a form of accountability to the community.

Before any dollar is spent or a new project launched, we owe it to our communities to pause and run the numbers. In local government, financial choices aren't simply about budgets; they're about consequences. When costs, obligations, or long-term impacts go unmeasured, overextension becomes inevitable.

Math may seem mundane, but it is one of the most potent tools of accountability. Done early and honestly, it can be a game-changer.

Spending the Public's Money

Every decision in local government is a spending decision. The question isn't *whether* we spend, it's *how, on what,* and *to what end.*

A critical distinction in public finance is the difference between consumption spending and investment spending—between short-term necessity and long-term value.

Consumption Spending

Consumption spending covers routine costs required to keep public services functioning, such as park mowing and maintenance, police and fire protection, street sweeping, and snow removal. These activities are essential to safety, cleanliness, and day-to-day quality of life, and they play a critical role in preserving assets and extending their useful life. The return on this spending is immediate and service-based: it sustains what exists rather than expanding capacity or generating compound value over time. When consumption costs grow faster than revenues, communities are forced into difficult tradeoffs—higher taxes, fewer services or declining quality that ultimately accelerates asset deterioration.

Investment Spending

Investment spending strengthens a community's financial position over time by generating revenue, reducing future costs, or both. These are the choices that create fiscal momentum. Examples include constructing facilities designed to produce revenues that exceed operating expenses, upgrading to energy-efficient park lighting to reduce long-term utility costs, or forming public–private partnerships to develop assets that generate net positive revenue. Unlike consumption spending, investment spending has a multiplier effect: money spent today yields benefits for years to come and can compound capacity rather than drain it.

The challenge is that consumption spending is often politically easier. It produces visible, immediate results. Investment spending requires foresight, patience, and discipline, but over time, sustainability depends on how intentionally communities balance the two.

Measuring What Matters

The conversation about how we spend public money ultimately leads to a more consequential question: how do we know whether those investments are actually delivering the intended impacts, both now and over time?

Return on Investment (ROI) and Social Return on Investment (SROI) provide practical frameworks for answering that question by translating intention into measurable outcomes and capturing value in both financial and social terms.

ROI measures financial return—how much revenue or cost savings result from an investment. It's the business discipline that ensures every dollar spent is working as hard as it can. For example, a full-service recreation and wellness center generating $1.5 million annually while incurring $1.3 million in operating and maintenance expenses yields a positive ROI. That margin, when reinvested, allows for contribution to the center's long-term maintenance needs and /or can sustain other essential services that cannot pay for themselves.

ROI isn't everything, but without it, nothing endures. It's what allows a system to breathe, reinvest, maintain, and adapt without constant crisis.

SROI broadens the lens by capturing the social benefits created when public funds are invested in people and places, including improved health, civic pride, neighborhood safety, and social connection. A playground may never pay for itself, but it pays society back in ways that matter deeply. SROI ensures we keep those benefits in view.

However, both ROI and SROI lose meaning when used as slogans rather than measurements. Too often, they become tools of justification for projects that appear noble but make little financial or social sense. When untethered from clearly defined costs, identifiable beneficiaries, realistic outcomes, and evidence of long-term impact, ROI and SROI function as language rather than analysis.

When Square Footage Becomes the Strategy

Across the country, public agencies have become known for building expansive recreation facilities—120,000 square feet or more—filled with wide corridors, oversized lobbies, and sprawling non-revenue spaces that contribute little to the system's financial sustainability.

Of those 120,000 square feet, 80,000 square feet generate potential revenue through fitness, aquatics, rentals, and other services. The remaining 40,000 square feet—entries, hallways, locker rooms, administrative offices, and "gathering areas"—represent perpetual cost. They're heated, cooled, cleaned, and staffed, yet generate no offsetting revenue.

This isn't good business sense; it's architectural vanity. The justification is often emotional—"we need a grand entry," "we're building a place for social gathering." But when asked for evidence that those spaces function as social hubs, most can't provide it or quietly admit they don't.

Meanwhile, private-sector operators are often cited with frustration: "How can they charge so little?" The answer is simpler than it sounds. Private operators design facilities and services around what users are willing and able to pay. They minimize nonproductive space, maximize revenue-generating areas, and align design with cost recovery. If they misjudge demand or operate inefficiently, users stop coming, and the business fails. There is no broader community or tax base to absorb the loss.

Parks and recreation should not emulate private business, but it must learn from it. Every square foot of a public building incurs a perpetual cost to taxpayers. When design decisions prioritize form or image over function, communities inherit a liability disguised as legacy.

Good design isn't about scale. It's about ensuring every square foot advances the mission and strengthens financial sustainability.

The Benefits of Doing Math

1. Strategic Clarity

Example: A proposed 120,000-square-foot community center carries a $50 million construction price tag. That figure dominates early conversations. But construction is only the entry cost. The real question is whether the facility can be *operated, maintained, and renewed over its full life*.

To answer that question, operating, maintenance, and major replacement costs were modeled over a 25-year period using a conservative 3.5 percent annual inflation assumption. This inflation rate does not reflect growth or expansion of the facility. It reflects the rising cost of labor, utilities, materials, and services over time. When those predictable cost increases are accounted for, the facility's total lifecycle cost approaches $136 million.

Facility Square Footage	120,000					
Construction Costs	$50,000,000					
CPI (Consumer Price Index)	3.5%					
Annual Operating Costs	**Year 1**	**Year 5**	**Year 10**	**Year 15**	**Year 20**	**Year 25**
- Ops & Maint (Total)	$2,000,000	$2,295,046	$2,725,795	$3,237,389	$3,845,003	$4,566,657
- Ops & Maint (per Sq Ft)	$16.67	$19.13	$22.71	$26.98	$32.04	$38.06
Replacement Costs	**Year 1**	**Year 5**	**Year 10**	**Year 15**	**Year 20**	**Year 25**
- HVAC	$2,400,000	$2,754,055	$3,270,954	$3,884,867	$4,614,003	$5,479,988
- Roof	$1,200,000	$1,377,028	$1,635,477	$1,942,433	$2,307,002	$2,739,994
- FF&E	$50,000	$57,376	$68,145	$80,935	$96,125	$114,166

The table illustrates how those costs unfold.

- Year 1 operating costs represent today's conditions: staffing, utilities, routine maintenance, custodial services, and basic upkeep required to keep the building open, safe, and functional.
- As the facility ages, operating and maintenance costs rise, not because service levels increase, but because wages grow, utilities cost more, materials inflate, and aging systems require more attention.
- Operating cost per square foot makes visible how scale compounds responsibility. Every square foot built

carries a recurring obligation, year after year, regardless of how heavily the space is used.

The replacement costs shown are not discretionary upgrades. They reflect core systems reaching the end of their useful life:

- HVAC systems must be replaced to maintain indoor air quality, safety, and code compliance.
- Roofs fail predictably and must be replaced to protect the building and the investment beneath them.
- Fixtures, furniture, and equipment (FF&E) wear out through daily use and must be renewed for the facility to remain functional and accessible.

These costs are not optional, and they are not signs of mismanagement. They are the natural consequence of owning and operating a building of this scale.

When all of these obligations are viewed together—construction, operations, maintenance, and replacement—the framing changes. The question is no longer *"Can we build it?"* but *"Can we afford to operate and maintain it over time?"*

That shift, from enthusiasm to endurance, is the value of doing the math.

2. Asset Preservation

Every playground, trail, and facility has a finite lifecycle. Materials wear, systems degrade, and safety standards evolve. Doing the math ensures replacement and reinvestment plans are in place before failure occurs, rather than after it disrupts service or forces emergency spending.

Example: Based on an approach used by the Glencoe (IL) Park District, the "heat sheet" illustrated here organizes an agency's playground inventory in a way that makes future capital obligations visible and actionable.

Parks & Recreation Facility and Asset Renewal Plan

NEW	New amenity not in our current inventory
3	Remaining useful life expected to be greater than 10 years
2	Amenity will need significant repairs, renovations or replacement in the next 4-10
1	Amenity is at or near the end of its useful life

Priority	Amenity	Install Date	Typical Useful Life (Years)	Condition Assessment Remaining Useful Life %	Current Replacment Cost (FY 25)	Estimated Replacement Year (FY XX)	Future Replacment Cost (5% CAGR)
	Playgrounds						
3	Playground A	2023	20	85%	$600,000	2043	$1,443,972
3	Playground B	2020	20	70%	$300,000	2040	$623,678
2	Playground C	2015	20	45%	$400,000	2035	$651,558
2	Playground D	2012	20	30%	$700,000	2032	$984,970
1	Playground E	2009	20	15%	$500,000	2029	$607,753
1	Playground F	2006	20	0%	$200,000	2026	$210,000
				Playground Total	$2,700,000		$4,521,931

The table does several important things at once:

- It identifies what assets exist, when they were installed, and their typical useful life.

- It pairs age with current condition, expressed as remaining useful life, so decision-makers can see which assets are stable, which are deteriorating, and which are approaching failure.
- Color coding highlights priority, drawing attention to assets that will require significant reinvestment in the near term rather than spreading attention evenly across the system.
- Replacement years make timing explicit, reducing the risk that multiple high-cost assets fail at once.

The Future Replacement Cost column projects the cost to replace each playground at the end of its useful life. This projection uses a five percent Compound Annual Growth Rate (CAGR) to reflect how construction and equipment costs tend to increase over time.

CAGR differs from a flat inflation assumption in one important way:

- Costs increase on top of prior increases, not from the original starting value.
- Over long periods, this compounding effect

significantly widens the gap between today's prices and future obligations.

In practical terms, this means that delaying reinvestment does not simply postpone cost; it amplifies it.

What the heat sheet ultimately provides is foresight. It allows agencies to:

- anticipate future capital needs,
- smooth reinvestment over time,
- avoid emergency replacements,
- and align funding strategies with actual asset condition rather than crisis.

Doing the math transforms asset preservation from a reactive problem into a manageable responsibility.

3. Service (program) Management

Every service comes with costs. Doing the math makes those costs visible and allows organizations to decide—intentionally—how services should be managed, funded and priced.

Tracking cost recovery compares the total revenue generated by a service to the total expense required to deliver it. This comparison does not determine whether a service is "good" or "bad." It clarifies the total cost of a service and the amount offset by revenues generated.

Example: The table illustrates a park and recreation department's effort to examine the cost recovery performance of its Camps and Out-of-School services by comparing revenues and expenses for each program type.

Service Category	Service Area	Sub Service Area	Total Revenue	Total Expense	Cost Recovery %
Enrichment & Non-Skilled Activities	Camps and Out-of-School	AM Club & Extra Innings	$ 276,455	$ 209,233	132%
Enrichment & Non-Skilled Activities	Camps and Out-of-School	Camp Discovery	$ 14,064	$ 40,521	35%
Enrichment & Non-Skilled Activities	Camps and Out-of-School	Days-Off School Camps	$ 32,069	$ 29,395	109%
Enrichment & Non-Skilled Activities	Camps and Out-of-School	Hobo Jungle Camps	$ 9,882	$ 20,362	49%
Enrichment & Non-Skilled Activities	Camps and Out-of-School	Recreation Camps	$ 13,216	$ 17,312	76%
Enrichment & Non-Skilled Activities	Camps and Out-of-School	Stomping Grounds	$ 167,900	$ 207,578	81%
Enrichment & Non-Skilled Activities	Camps and Out-of-School	Teen Camp	$ 53,870	$ 82,448	65%

What the table reveals:

- Services with cost recovery above 100 percent generate more revenue than they cost to operate. In these cases, user fees fully cover expenses and may help offset costs elsewhere in the system.
- Services with cost recovery below 100 percent rely on public subsidy to operate. The gap between revenue and expense represents taxpayer support.

- The variation across programs highlights that Camps and Out-of-School services are not a single financial category. Different formats, durations, staffing models, and audiences produce very different cost structures and recovery outcomes.

This information shifts the conversation from assumption to intention.

Instead of asking *"Can we afford this program?"* the questions become:

- Which services are essential because they protect safety, access, or developmental outcomes?
- Which services justify subsidy because they deliver a broad community benefit?
- Which services could be right-sized, restructured, or repriced to better align cost and value?
- And which services may no longer warrant continuation in their current form?

Cost recovery analysis does not prescribe answers. It provides clarity.

When organizations do not examine service-level performance, subsidies occur by default. When they do, subsidy becomes a deliberate choice, aligned with purpose and the common good.

The Consequences of Ignoring Math

Ignoring math, relying on flawed assumptions, or pursuing projects without financial discipline leads to predictable outcomes. Across communities of every size, the same three patterns appear.

1. <u>Neglecting Ongoing Maintenance and Operations</u>

   Ribbon cuttings happen without identified long-term funding for operations or preventive maintenance. Fees may increase, or new charges may be introduced, creating the expectation that facilities will be reliable and well cared for. Instead, assets age and systems fail sooner than anticipated. From the public's perspective, the result is straightforward: they paid more for something that works less. Over time, this gap between promise and performance erodes trust, not just in the facility, but in the organization's stewardship of public resources.

2. Misreading Long-Term Costs

New developments bring short-term excitement and visible progress, but they often obscure future liabilities. Construction costs are treated as the primary hurdle, while ongoing operations, maintenance, and eventual replacement are minimized. Those obligations do not disappear. They accumulate, shifting costs and risks to future budgets, leaders, and residents. What feels affordable today becomes a structural burden tomorrow.

3. Synchronized Decay

When multiple facilities are built or renovated simultaneously, they age together. Roofs, mechanical systems, and major components reach the end of their useful lives in rapid succession, creating a funding cliff in which multiple high-cost replacements are required simultaneously. Without advanced planning and reserves, organizations are forced into reactive decisions—deferral, debt, or emergency appeals—rather than orderly reinvestment.

Without rigorous analysis and discipline, progress becomes a cycle of build, defer, repair, and borrow. Math always catches up. The only question is whether communities confront it early or pay for it later.

Debt and the Illusion of Capacity

"Debt is normal. That's just how government works." I've heard that line far too many times. Debt itself isn't the problem; it's dependence on it that is.

Used thoughtfully, debt can be a responsible tool. It allows communities to build long-lasting facilities and spread costs across generations who benefit from them. But over time, some governments stop treating debt as a tool and start treating it as a habit. They assume that if something can be financed, it can be afforded, a dangerous confusion between cash flow and capacity. The numbers may look balanced on paper, but real costs lurk beneath.

Debt used this way doesn't build strength; it hides fragility. Like putting expenses on a credit card every month, it works until it doesn't.

Healthy governments don't swear off debt altogether, but they use it strategically. They borrow for long-term value and fund operations with recurring, reliable revenue streams.

Case in Point: The Tournament Sports Complex

Parks and recreation systems often justify mega sports complexes by citing their potential Return on Investment (ROI), Social Return on Investment (SROI), and benefits such as increased family visits, spending at hotels and restaurants, and a boost in civic pride. These claims are attractive and, in the abstract, persuasive. But without careful attention to ROI and long-term capital costs, SROI arguments collapse under the weight of math.

Consider a tournament-style sports complex in Florida that opened with roughly $1.13 million in reserves. Its annual operations generated a $150,000 return that, at first glance, looked sustainable. But when future capital cost projections were factored in, the picture changed dramatically:

- Four years from opening: projected $1.85 million in turf replacement > reserves balance falls to –$120,000.
- Seven years from opening: projected $1.69 million for parking and partial lighting > reserves balance drops to –$1.36 million.
- Thirteen years from opening: projected $2.42 million for another round of turf

replacement >reserves balance plummets to –$2.9 million.

These figures do account for the presumed compounding of maintenance investments, but don't account for other infrastructure obligations, such as water, sidewalks, and road maintenance. Even with a steady $150,000 annual return, the facility quickly becomes a long-term liability.

This is where ROI and SROI must be weighed against each other. The SROI case for the complex might emphasize youth opportunities, community branding, and the promise of economic tourism impacts, but when ROI cannot keep pace with capital reinvestment needs, those assumed social benefits come at the expense of the commons—neighborhood parks, playgrounds, and everyday infrastructure that residents rely on.

The uncomfortable but necessary question is this: *What if the community had chosen not to build?* Yes, it would have forgone the $150,000 annual return and the intangible benefits of hosting tournaments. But it would also have avoided tens of millions in capital costs, mounting deficits, and a future in which taxpayers are forced to subsidize a specialized facility used by relatively few.

The tournament complex example shows why ROI must be prioritized if financial sustainability is the goal. SROI adds value, but when used as a stand-alone justification, it becomes dangerous rhetoric that overextends systems and leaves future generations with debt instead of opportunity.

Checks & Balances: Questions That Should Have Been Asked Before Building

When evaluating any major capital project, especially those justified by promises of tourism or "economic impact", communities should pause and ask a small set of grounding questions.

<u>1. ROI Reality Check</u>

Return on Investment (ROI) asks whether a project can pay for itself—not just in its early years, but over its full lifecycle.

- Does projected revenue cover day-to-day operations and long-term capital reinvestment?
- How much of the revenue is predictable versus dependent on continued demand?

Applied to the tournament complex:

The facility generated an annual operating surplus

of roughly $150,000, positive on paper. But that surplus was nowhere near sufficient to absorb predictable capital costs such as turf replacement, parking rehabilitation, and lighting upgrades. Once those costs were introduced, the project's ROI turned negative, despite steady operations.

2. SROI Reality Check

Social Return on Investment (SROI) focuses on claimed community benefits that do not appear on a balance sheet.

- What social outcomes are promised?
- Who experiences those benefits, and how often?

Applied to the tournament complex:

Supporters emphasized youth opportunity, community pride, and tourism exposure. Yet access was largely limited to tournament participants and travel teams. Residents who ultimately absorbed the financial risk saw little direct benefit relative to cost.

3. Tourism & Spending Math

Economic impact claims often highlight gross spending without examining where value accrues.

- Who captures visitor spending—locals, national chains, or private operators?
- How much of that spending returns to the public entity responsible for the facility?

Applied to the tournament complex:

Families stayed in hotels and ate at restaurants, but only a small fraction of that spending flowed back to the local government system through fees or taxes. Meanwhile, the full cost of maintaining and replacing the facility remained a public obligation.

4. Opportunity Cost

Every major investment consumes capacity—financial, operational, and political.

- What does this project displace?
- What maintenance, staffing, or neighborhood investments are deferred as a result?

Applied to the tournament complex:

As reserves declined, the pressure to subsidize the facility increased. Dollars that could have supported playground replacement, trail repairs, or park maintenance were redirected to keep a specialized, tournament-driven asset operational.

5. The "What If" Question

Declining to build is also a strategic decision.

- What flexibility would be preserved by not moving forward?
- What alternative investments could advance broader community benefit with less risk?

Applied to the tournament complex:

By choosing not to build, the community would have forgone tournament hosting and modest annual returns, but it also would have avoided recurring capital shortfalls, long-term deficits, and the eventual need to subsidize a facility serving a narrow user base.

There's a myth that math is cold, clinical, or bureaucratic. In reality, math is deeply human. It's an act of respect and honor for those who pay for and rely on public services.

CHAPTER 14

DOING BETTER WITH WHAT WE HAVE

> "We've run out of money. It's time to start thinking."
>
> – Earnest Rutherford, Physicist

Decisions to spend public dollars are declarations of what matters, who matters, and how we see our role in shaping the community's future. Yet decision-making in local government, particularly within parks and recreation and other quality-of-life services, often drifts toward short-term urgency, political convenience, or vocal pressure rather than principled reasoning.

Former Pasadena, California, Mayor Rick Cole once said, "A budget is a moral document." It is more than a spreadsheet or statutory requirement; it is a blueprint of priorities in action. Budgets reveal what we value and what we choose to elevate, preserve, defer, or deny. How we allocate resources speaks louder than any mission statement. Do we maintain what we have or chase what looks new? Do we support equitable access or cater to influence? Do we fund what's right or what's loudest?

A moral budget requires integrity. Fiscal responsibility and social responsibility are inseparable. Every public dollar is a tool of service.

The Cost of Fragmentation

Many in public service enter with the best intentions, yet over time, a gap emerges between what organizations say they value and how decisions are made. Agencies claim equity while approving projects that benefit the few. They celebrate new development while deferring maintenance on aging facilities. The problem lies less in people than in systems that reward visibility over alignment and long-term value. Those disconnects arise from how organizations are structured and how planning efforts take shape.

This misalignment extends beyond any single agency or form of government. In special districts, including park, library, and fire protection districts, the same tensions arise. Separate boards, independent taxing authorities, and distinct operational mandates can create internal silos just as rigid as those in municipal government.

Fragmentation across the broader civic landscape only magnifies the challenge. Municipal departments operate as their own enterprises—Parks and Recreation develops a master plan, Public Works crafts an infrastructure plan, Housing prepares an affordability strategy, Police build a safety plan, and Planning produces a comprehensive plan. Each may be thoughtfully constructed, yet few truly connect. Meanwhile, special districts often develop parallel plans, creating multiple layers of strategy, each valuable but rarely integrated. Communities don't fail for lack of plans; they falter when those plans fail to speak to one another.

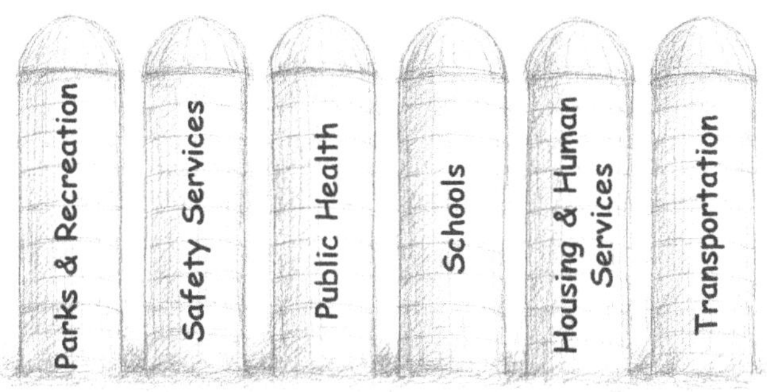

When municipal departments and districts act in isolation, opportunities disappear in the gaps between them. Housing insecurity, public safety, mental health, access to green space, climate resilience, and economic mobility are interconnected challenges. Fragmentation multiplies inefficiency and conceals the costs of disconnection.

Simply put, integrated planning reflects how durable systems function: through alignment and collective action. Whether in a municipal department or a special district, it requires the collective "we" to work across silos and move toward a shared vision and shared responsibility for community well-being.

Integration is Optimization

Optimization expresses intentional alignment in action. It asks: *What impact are we trying to have?* When departments agree on shared outcomes before designing separate projects, they make better use of public resources. A single facility can serve as a library, public health hub, and recreation center. A coordinated maintenance team can care for both streetscapes and parks when service standards are clear. Infrastructure staff can manage asset lifecycles and long-term maintenance across systems rather than in silos.

This approach doesn't require more money; it requires clearer coordination, shared responsibility, and intentional design. Effective organizations curate what they do through purpose and coordinated effort. Doing better with what we have often requires rethinking rather than reducing.

Clarity of purpose safeguards quality. The healthiest systems know their lane and understand how it connects to others. Systems perform best when leaders know when to lead, when to follow, and when to merge.

Budgeting for Outcomes

Budgeting for outcomes begins by defining impact before determining services and allocating expenditures. Traditional budgeting answers the question, “What can we fund?” Budgeting for outcomes asks, “What impacts are we trying to have?” It reverses the order of operations by prioritizing community outcomes, then aligning resources and measures of success to achieve them.

When done well, this approach connects every dollar to a purpose. It forces clarity around what matters most and exposes whether current spending advances those goals. It transforms budgets from accounting tools into design instruments.

Imagine if a city recognized youth obesity as a community-wide issue that intersects multiple departments and organizations—parks and recreation, public health, housing, schools, and local nonprofits. Instead of each entity pursuing its own strategies, they could align their existing budgets toward a single measurable outcome: increasing daily physical activity and nutrition among local youth.

Parks and recreation could expand access to nearby parks through joint-use agreements with schools and integrate physical activity into after-school programs. The school district might reintroduce structured recess during the day. The public health department could track wellness and behavioral data to measure progress. The housing department might invest in neighborhood design, safe routes, and play areas that encourage active living. Local nonprofits could provide outreach, education, and family engagement.

The impact could have broader implications. Children could be healthier and more focused in school. Neighborhoods could be safer and more connected. Families could have more opportunities to move, play, and learn together. Dollars could stretch further because every investment would contribute to a shared purpose rather than isolated efforts.

Budgeting for outcomes reframes the conversation from cost to consequence and from activity to impact. It is the financial expression of discipline—aligning money with meaning and ensuring that every expenditure advances the common good.

Integration builds coherence. It amplifies expertise through connection. When housing, transportation, parks, public safety, and others coordinate their plans, they create leverage that no single organization can achieve on its own. Through alignment, cities shift from fragmentation to collaboration, and from doing more to doing better.

CHAPTER 15

POLICY IS POWER

> "It's hard to imagine a domain of public life that isn't affected by public policy."
>
> – William Howell

We talk often about vision, values, and leadership, but nothing gives those ideas weight like policy. Policy is how a community says, *"This is how we do things here."* It is how intentions survive personalities and how discipline outlives pressure.

When crafted with care, policy becomes the backbone of stewardship—largely unseen, but essential to keeping the system upright when the pressure is on. It's what keeps a city, a district, or a department from losing its way when the winds of politics shift or when budgets tighten. Policy doesn't exist to limit us. It provides guardrails.

The Backbone of Stewardship

Think of policy as the spine that supports the body

of local government's work–budgets, projects, programs, and decisions–keeping it upright and aligned. Without it, good intentions sag under the weight of convenience, and principles bend toward whoever is loudest that week.

Policy is the difference between hoping we stay on course and designing a way to make sure we do. It gives professional staff confidence, helps elected officials act with consistency and clarity, and provides the community with assurance that decisions are guided by purpose rather than politics.

Every organization has stories of when policy protected them–when a clear cost-recovery policy or partnership guideline prevented a hasty decision or a political favor. Those moments happen when good judgment is codified.

What Policy Really Does

Policy is more than paper; it's a promise. It removes guesswork by turning values into expectations and principles into practice. For staff, it clarifies what "right" looks like when decisions are difficult. For elected officials, it anchors choices in shared standards rather than personal preference. And for residents, it builds trust in the process–even when they don't love the outcome.

When policy is clear, we spend less time reacting and more time leading. It translates abstract ideas like accountability into everyday behaviors. It creates fairness through consistency and courage through clarity.

Policies make invisible values visible. They say, *"We don't waive fees without cause. We don't add new facilities until we can maintain the ones we have. We don't make promises without a way to keep them."* That's integrity in writing.

Without policy, organizations adopt improvisation. Fees get set on emotion. Exceptions multiply. Priorities blur. What begins as flexibility quickly becomes inequity, with some people benefiting because they asked, while others lose out because they didn't know they could.

In the absence of policy, consistency becomes personality-driven. When expectations are unwritten, outcomes depend on who occupies a role rather than on shared standards. Decisions shift with elections or new administrations, not because the community's values have changed, but because there is nothing anchoring them.

The system becomes fragile because it relies on people rather than principles. Professionals may learn to wait out elected officials or adapt defensively. Financial discipline gives way to survival, and public trust erodes as decisions feel unpredictable.

Policy as an Ethical Act

Policy is how a government demonstrates its values and those of the community it serves.

A financial sustainability policy tells the truth about cost. A capital investment policy tells the truth about limits. An equity policy tells the truth about who's been left out and what to do about it.

When adopted, these policies create discipline not just for today's decisions but for decades to come. They outlast elections and egos. They remind everyone, from staff to council members to residents, that stewardship isn't situational. It's systemic.

Good policy also invites connection. It ties local decisions to the broader common good. It aligns the daily choices of one department with the long-term health of the entire organization. It reminds us that financial responsibility is more than balancing budgets. It's about the integrity of decisions behind every tax dollar spent.

Policy as Protection

In the most challenging moments—when a beloved service faces cuts or when someone demands a special exception—policy is what allows us to say no with confidence and conviction. It shifts decisions from personal judgment to shared commitment. It's not a personal rejection; it's a principled one.

Policy is often misunderstood as a list of rules. Good policy is more nuanced. It establishes intent, boundaries, and responsibility. It clarifies why decisions are made, rather than merely what is allowed or prohibited. Rules can guide behavior, but policy provides the framework that makes judgment consistent and defensible.

Policy is the quiet ally that allows professionals to stand firm under pressure. It is how organizations navigate political terrain without losing their footing. And it only works when the people responsible for carrying it out understand it, trust it, and apply it thoughtfully in daily decisions.

When I worked for the city of Boulder, Colorado, a young lifeguard, earnest, well-intentioned, and new to the job, told a woman she couldn't breastfeed on the pool deck because "we don't allow food and beverages on the deck." He wasn't trying to cause harm; he was enforcing what he believed was policy.

But there was no policy prohibiting breastfeeding. What existed was an operational rule about food and beverages, applied without context or clarity. The result was not protection, but harm, caused not by malice, but by ambiguity. When policy is unclear or absent, people fill the gaps themselves.

Clarity protects staff just as much as it protects the public. When expectations are clearly articulated—what the organization stands for, what it permits, and where discretion applies—decision-making becomes consistent and defensible rather than reactive or personal.

Clarity also allows courage to compound. When one policy is applied thoughtfully and upheld, it sets a precedent. Over time, those precedents serve as guardrails and shared understandings.

At its core, policy is how an organization keeps its promises to the community. Services may evolve, leadership may turn over, and budgets may tighten, but well-crafted policy holds. It is the scaffolding that allows responsible governance to stand, even when pressure mounts.

PART IV: RENEWAL
THE PATH FORWARD

After the storm passes, survival is not enough.

Renewal depends on discernment—what to restore, what to release, and what must be carried forward with greater care over time. The herd does not return unchanged; it adapts, informed by what endured and what did not.

In public service, renewal is built through collective will and the judgment to do good work consistently. Transformation is rarely dramatic. It takes shape through disciplined decisions, ethical leadership, and a long view that extends beyond individual tenure or political cycles.

The path forward is not marked by optimism alone, but by tenacity and purpose. Renewal is sustained by the discipline to uphold clear boundaries, learn from experience, and remain accountable to both present needs and those yet to come.

CHAPTER 16
INSPIRING COLLECTIVE WILL

> "Unless someone like you cares a whole awful lot, nothing is going to get better. It's not."
>
> – Dr. Seuss, The Lorax

Caring is the catalyst. But in public parks and recreation, it just isn't enough. If we want to build systems that last, we must do more than love our work. We must lead people toward understanding. We must turn empathy into education and passion into persuasion.

Persuasion as a Public Service

Persuasion in government is not manipulation. It's a civic responsibility. It is how truth becomes understandable, how data becomes direction, and how a community learns to see itself not as customers, but as co-owners of the common good.

To persuade well is to care deeply—to explain, to

contextualize, to translate complexity into clarity. The work isn't to convince people that we're right, but to help them *see why it matters* and *how they belong in it*.

People rarely resist change because they are stubborn. They resist it because they don't understand it, and they don't understand it because we too often fail to explain why it's happening.

The Power of *Because*

In the late 1970s, Harvard researcher Ellen Langer discovered something profound yet straightforward: people are far more likely to support an action when they're given a reason, even a small one. Simply, the word *because* can bridge the gap between policy and purpose.

In public service, it sounds like this:

We increased the fee *because* it allows us to keep the program running without lowering quality.

We're reinvesting in existing parks *because* it's more responsible than expanding into areas we can't maintain.

Every 'because' carries a signal of respect. It tells people they are worthy of the truth. It replaces suspicion with understanding, and obligation with ownership.

Transparent Criteria, Trustworthy Systems

Clarity builds confidence. When the reasoning behind decisions is transparent, when people can see the criteria that shape priorities, trust grows.

Communities respond differently when they understand why something was chosen.

Because it aligns with the master plan they helped create.

Because it serves more than a few.

Because we want to focus on maintaining what we have rather than overextending the community's resources.

Without clarity guideposts, decision-making looks arbitrary. With them, it seems principled. Transparency doesn't eliminate disappointment, but it softens it with understanding.

Every audience in this work carries its own fears and motivations. Elected officials may worry about popularity and re-election. Residents may focus on personal wants and what feels fair. Staff may see the world through their daily tasks and their silos.

When people understand the larger system they're part of, their questions change from *"What do I get?"* or *"How does this affect me?"* to *"What makes sense for us?"*

Collective movement rarely happens because everyone agrees on every step. It happens when enough of the group understands the direction and moves in rhythm. Progress depends less on unanimity than on shared signals and an understanding that staying oriented to the whole matters more than individual comfort or benefit.

This is the moment persuasion becomes collective understanding.

The way we communicate choices often matters more than the choices themselves. A poorly framed question can turn an opportunity into an argument, while a well-framed one can turn skepticism into support. Framing is not about spin; it's about honesty. It's about helping people see the whole picture before they're asked to decide.

Consider an organization that has just completed a community survey. For many communities, surveys are among the most visible and trusted means by which residents are invited into decision-making. They are often treated as a proxy for collective will, a way of translating public input into direction, priorities, and perceived mandate.

In this case, the survey results appear to indicate that residents overwhelmingly want a new pool. Excitement builds. The headline writes itself. The survey is cited as evidence that the community has spoken.

But what the data doesn't reveal is just as important as what it shows. Surveys can capture desire, but they rarely capture tradeoffs. They don't automatically reflect willingness or ability to pay, nor do they surface how priorities shift when costs, impacts, or alternatives are made explicit. Without that context, what appears to be consensus can quickly become conflict.

That's where framing matters. How we ask questions determines the answers we get.

"Are you in favor of a new pool?"

"Would you support a new pool with your taxpayer dollars?"

"Would you support a new pool if it raised your taxes by $108 a year and required admission fees to cover maintenance?"

Each version of the question pulls the curtain back a little further.

From Engagement to Education

We often confuse asking for opinions with building understanding.

Engagement tells us what people *desire*.

Education helps them grasp what's *possible*.

Persuasion connects both to *purpose*.

Input without context can quickly become data without wisdom. The goal is not to collect answers, but to cultivate awareness.

When we educate before we ask, we elevate the conversation from preference to principle. People begin to see beyond their front yard to the ecosystem that sustains them. They begin to understand that every dollar, every acre, every decision is part of a larger covenant between today and tomorrow.

I was reminded of this recently in my own community. A well-intentioned resident has been advocating tirelessly for a new ice rink—a vision born of love for our mountain town and for the joy it could bring local families. But our community cannot afford it. We are small, our infrastructure is stretched, and our maintenance backlog is growing. When I shared that reality, his reply came fast and sharp: *"So, you want to deprive our kids?"*

Several years earlier, I had written an Op-Ed intended for our local paper. Out of respect, I chose instead to send it directly to each city council member. The piece later evolved into an article titled *Ice Would Be Nice, But What About the Common Good.* It examined long-term obligation, fiscal capacity, and the cumulative impact of commitments that feel reasonable in isolation but compound over time.

Nearly two years later, I received an email from the vice president of a local organization advocating for an ice rink. He requested a meeting to educate me on the project's importance. It was clear his intent was to convince me that my perspective was flawed.

I declined out of principle.

That decision was not in opposition to the idea itself. It was about boundaries. I had already stated my concerns publicly and transparently. A private conversation would not change the math, nor the broader obligations facing the community.

The response that followed was telling. In a subsequent message, he warned that he did not want to “embarrass” me because my perspective was inaccurate. Disagreement was reframed not as a difference in priorities, but as a personal failing.

That moment clarified something essential.

Special interests are often committed, organized, and sincere. But sincerity does not equal responsibility for the system as a whole. Advocacy carries passion; local government carries obligation.

What troubled me was not the request for a meeting, nor the attempt to persuade. It was the assumption that pressure should be applied personally, and disagreement treated as ignorance rather than a legitimate concern for long-term impact.

This is how civic decision-making becomes distorted, not through malice, but through the quiet privileging of organized interests over shared responsibility. When pressure replaces deliberation, the common good gives way to narrower aims.

Fiscal reality does not bend to enthusiasm. Long-term obligations do not disappear because a project is popular. Communities that allow private interests to define public priorities eventually inherit costs that were never fully debated or collectively owned.

This is why decisions must remain public, grounded,

and accountable to the whole. Not detached, but disciplined. Local government is not responsible for fulfilling every aspiration. It is responsible for protecting the conditions that allow a community to endure.

Words Matter

When we talk about fees, costs, and taxes, we aren't talking about punishment; we're talking about shared protection. Public parks and facilities remain open to all. Specialized or high-impact services require fees not because access is being denied, but because those who benefit directly help sustain what benefits everyone indirectly.

When people understand *why*, they stop hearing "fee" and start to hear "fair" or "just".

That's the language of shared responsibility.

Inspiring Collective Will

If we want a collective stand behind hard choices, we can't stop at sharing *what* we're doing. We must explain *why*. We must make the work visible, understandable, and shared. Informed communities make better decisions, and inspired communities protect what matters.

CHAPTER 17

JUDGMENT & DURABILITY

> "Wisdom is not knowing what to do next. It is knowing what matters most."
>
> – Anonymous

Public service is not short on good intentions. People enter this work because they care about their communities—about opportunity, fairness, and leaving things better than they found them. Concern, empathy, and commitment are abundant. These qualities are not scarce resources. And yet, systems still fail.

They fail not because people do not care enough, but because care alone cannot carry an organization through moments of complexity. There are times in public life when values compete, expectations collide, and consequences cannot be avoided. In those moments, intention offers no clear path forward. Judgment does.

In this context, judgment does not mean authority, instinct, or decisiveness for its own sake. It means choosing in ways the organization can stand behind when conditions change, and outcomes disappoint. Judgment is visible not in what is promised, but in what an institution consistently chooses to protect, prioritize, and preserve over time, especially when doing so is unpopular.

Organizations that rely on individual judgment depend on experience, temperament, and personal courage. Organizations that embed judgment into systems through policy, shared standards, and consistent practice build something different: durability.

When judgment lives primarily in individuals, it is fragile. When embedded in systems, it becomes durable and remains stable even as people, conditions, and expectations change.

Durability is not about resisting change or absorbing endless strain. It is about whether decisions are anchored and defensible. Whether commitments survive leadership turnover. Whether boundaries hold when expectations escalate. Durable organizations do not ask people to compensate for ambiguity; they design clarity, so people are not forced to improvise. Organizational judgment becomes less personal, less reactive, and less dependent on who happens to be in the room.

When judgment is not carried by the organization, it migrates. It shows up first among front-line staff and middle managers—those closest to the work and farthest from formal authority. Newer staff are asked to interpret priorities before they have context. Middle managers are responsible for implementation but often excluded from direction-setting, left to translate ambiguity upward and downward. Over time, they absorb frustration, are forced to explain decisions they did not shape, and enforce boundaries that were never clearly defined.

This fragility is felt most acutely by those early in their careers. The young coordinator, planner, analyst, or supervisor who enters public service with energy and conviction is often the first to encounter the consequences of unclear judgment. Asked to enforce rules that shift, explain decisions that feel inconsistent, and navigate expectations that change with the audience, they begin to learn, sometimes incorrectly, what the organization truly values.

Too often, they are placed in these conditions without the preparation, context, or institutional support needed to develop sound judgment. What fills the gap is not discernment, but habit: inherited practices, unspoken norms, and cultural narratives that normalize improvisation and ambiguity as "how we've always done it." I know this because I was that young coordinator—well-intentioned, eager to please, and willing to go along with long-standing cultural narratives rather than question the judgment of a system I assumed knew better than I did.

In systems where judgment is improvised rather than embedded, these early experiences do not build confidence or discernment. They build caution. Workarounds. Quiet disengagement. Over time, this shapes how people see public service itself, not as a place to grow judgment and responsibility, but as a place where clarity is scarce, and consequences are unevenly shared.

Concern about the future of local government is not rooted in a lack of purpose or relevance. It reflects something more practical and more solvable: whether public institutions are designed to support judgment consistently, so people can grow into responsibility rather than absorb friction created by its absence.

The effects extend beyond the organization. Community members experience unclear judgment as an inconsistency—rules that shift, decisions that seem unpredictable, and outcomes that are difficult to understand or to trust. Elected and appointed officials are drawn into operational questions not because they seek control, but because the organization has not provided a stable governance framework. In the absence of shared judgment, decisions become personalized, and political pressure fills the space where organizational clarity should reside.

I have seen what happens when judgment is clearly named and carried by the organization rather than absorbed quietly by individuals.

I was invited to facilitate a program on fiscal stewardship and long-term sustainability for parks and recreation professionals in a city in Nevada, followed by a separate session with the City Council, Parks and Recreation Commissioners, and County Commissioners.

At the conclusion of the professional staff training, I asked participants to write down what they believed would most likely get in the way of doing the important work they believed necessary. Many responses were candid. A significant number of responses pointed to appointed and elected officials who they believed would not support doing what was hard, but needed.

When the joint session with elected and appointed officials concluded the following day, the Parks and Recreation Director walked to the front of the room. He did not posture or soften his message. He spoke plainly.

He explained that I had asked staff what would stand in the way of them doing the work they believed needed to be done, and he shared what had been written. Then he spoke truth to power. If the department was going to do what was necessary, he needed governance to work with him and staff, and not against them. He needed alignment, not interference. Partnership, not contradiction. And he needed room to apply judgment grounded in long-term responsibility rather than short-term politics.

The room went quiet.

Then something important happened. The elected officials nodded. They acknowledged that support and advocacy were required if the system was going to endure. That moment illustrated something essential about judgment in public service. It is not about resisting authority or challenging people. It is about naming the truth of the system *in front of the system itself*—and doing so in a way that invites alignment rather than defensiveness.

Ambiguity does more than burden people; it invites people to participate in the problem. Staff rely on workarounds instead of standards. Managers buffer conflict instead of enforcing boundaries. Officials intervene in individual cases rather than strengthening systems. None of this stems from ill intent. But together, these behaviors normalize circumvention and weaken the organization's ability to act coherently.

This is how culture forms—through what is rehearsed and reinforced over time. Values rarely fail because people forget them. They fail because they were never practiced. In public service, values are quietly shaped by what is rewarded, tolerated, and accepted when decisions disappoint.

Organizations that rely on values only when controversy arises often discover too late that values cannot be summoned on demand. Judgment depends on habits formed when the stakes are lower.

Consider an organization that routinely grants exceptions in the name of responsiveness. Each accommodation feels justified. Each decision appears compassionate. Over time, the value being practiced is not care; it is the avoidance of boundaries. When conditions change, that same organization struggles to say no, not because it lacks values, but because it has trained itself to bypass them.

By contrast, organizations that consistently apply standards, honestly name trade-offs, and use policy to clarify rather than obscure, build cultures in which judgment is understood and embraced rather than resisted. In these systems, values do not need to be debated when tension arises; they are already embedded in how decisions are made.

This is how values become usable—not as ideals to reference, but as operating standards that guide behavior over time, across roles, and through leadership transitions.

Wisdom in public service is often mistaken for reflection or patience. In practice, it looks more like strength. The strength to establish boundaries before they are tested. The strength to explain decisions when doing so is uncomfortable. The strength to protect the integrity of the system even when outcomes disappoint.

This kind of strength rarely draws attention. It does not produce immediate wins. It shows up quietly through continuity, credibility, and trust that compound over time. Organizations that possess it do not depend on exceptional people to rescue them in difficult moments. They rely on systems designed to ensure consistent judgment.

Judgment can often feel like restraint, uncertainty, and standing firm when movement is easier. But judgment is the threshold through which transformation must pass. Without it, change becomes motion without direction. With it, organizations gain the capacity to evolve without unraveling, to adapt without improvising, and to move forward without abandoning what must be honored.

CHAPTER 18
TRANSFORMATION

> "Power properly understood is nothing but the ability to achieve purpose. It is the strength required to bring about social, political, and economic change."
>
> – Martin Luther King

Imagine a community that does more than survive disruption—one that becomes more capable because of it—balancing aspiration with capacity, compassion with accountability, and growth with care.

Transformation begins after judgment has been exercised. After responsibility replaces reaction. After clarity replaces improvisation. After courage replaces conformity.

Communities do not change because of vision statements or momentary resolve. They change because the organizations within them decide to operate differently; consistently, deliberately, and in service of the common good. The health of a community reflects the discipline of its institutions. If we want resilient communities, we must first build organizations capable of holding complexity without unraveling.

Future-ready organizations do not wait for certainty or comfort. Like bison facing a storm, they adopt a posture of strength—grounded, forward-leaning, and informed by experience. They do not rush blindly ahead, nor do they scatter in search of relief. They move with discipline because the system depends on it. These organizations understand what matters most.

They understand that education is not an accessory to governance, but its foundation. People cannot support what they do not understand. Transparency is not a courtesy, but a responsibility. Explaining cost, tradeoffs, and consequences is how trust is built—not after decisions are made, but before expectations harden.

They understand that quality-of-life services are not peripheral. Parks, open spaces, recreation, and community infrastructure are public health systems. They shape how people move, connect, recover, and belong. Designing for everyday use is how communities become healthier, more resilient, and more equitable over time.

They understand that resources are finite, and discipline is not optional. Financial sustainability is not achieved through reaction, but through deliberate design. Assets must be cared for before new ones are added. Revenue must be diversified. Subsidy must be aligned with public benefit rather than popularity. Growth without capacity is not progress; it's ultimate failure.

They understand that partnerships are tools, not solutions. Collaboration works only when risk is shared, incentives are aligned, and purpose is clear. Otherwise, complexity multiplies and accountability dissolves.

They understand that saying no is sometimes the most responsible act of leadership. Not every demand deserves a yes. Not every idea merits investment. Protecting the system often requires disappointing individuals and being willing to explain why.

They understand that access is strengthened by lifting baseline conditions. Directing investment toward communities with fewer options improves outcomes for everyone. Equity is not achieved through equal distribution, but through deliberate attention to need, impact, and long-term stability.

They understand that what gets measured signals what matters. Outcomes outweigh outputs. Health, connection, learning, and resilience matter more than attendance counts or square footage.

Just as important, future-ready organizations understand what to resist. They resist the pull of popularity in favor of purpose. They resist overbuilding without funding. They resist specialization that serves the few at the expense of the many. And, they resist silence when clarity is needed most.

Transformation does not belong to those who cling to what is familiar. It belongs to those willing to think critically, act with discipline, and steward systems they may never personally benefit from.

The community we need is a choice.

A choice to trade comfort for courage.
A choice to trade familiarity for accountability.
A choice to do what lasts, not just what feels good.

The differentiators are clear.
The work is demanding.
And the moment will always be now.

FINAL CHAPTER

TENACITY & PURPOSE

Storms test not only the endurance of systems but the discipline of the people responsible for leading them. Yet storms also clarify and strip away illusion, leaving only what was designed to last.

When the clouds gather and the wind turns cold, bison do not scatter or search for shelter. They lower their heads and move forward together. They understand what we too often forget—that storms must be faced.

Public stewardship, at its best, must carry that same wisdom into practice. The future will not belong to those who wait for better conditions. It will belong to those who faced the headwinds when it mattered with eyes wide open, structures in place, guided by principle and grounded in the common good.

Because the work was never about weathering a single storm, it has always been about building something that could withstand all of them.

That is our charge—to design communities, institutions, and lives that endure not by accident, but with intention. To replace comfort with courage, consumption with contribution, and motion with meaning.

Every generation will face its own storm, and every one of us will decide whether to wait it out or walk into it.

The question before us is not whether we can survive it, but whether we'll leave a legacy that can.

ACKNOWLEDGEMENTS

This book is the result of years of experience, reflection, and relentless questioning—and it was not created alone. Every chapter carries the imprint of people who walked this journey with me. It is the culmination of many conversations, honest critiques, and steady encouragement offered along the way.

Those who traveled alongside me, whether for a moment or for miles, helped surface blind spots and push The Bison Principle to become what it needed to be. Though the book bears my name, it was shaped, strengthened, and steadied by many voices. In that sense, it reflects not only my convictions but the generosity, wisdom, and care of those who contributed to it.

This work has been shaped by practitioners and thinkers who examine public finance, land use, sustainable growth, and civic engagement as real-world systems with real consequences.

Dr. Andrew (Andy) Mowen's research was formative. His work on the Great Recession's impact on parks and recreation documented a widening structural gap between operating revenues and expenditures, revealing how expanding service menus often occur at the expense of reinvesting in existing infrastructure. His scholarship gave language to what many professionals continue to experience but struggle to articulate: systemic imbalance.

That same reality is echoed in the work of Strong Towns and in the book *Strong Towns* by Charles (Chuck) Marohn. Their work sharpened my understanding of how well-intended growth can quietly undermine long-term stability. Strong Towns' focus on incremental development and financial resilience reinforced the importance of building systems that communities can afford.

This discipline is further reinforced through Kevin Shepherd and Verdunity, whose analyses demonstrate that land-use decisions and financial outcomes are inseparable. Their work makes visible what is too often hidden: the long-term fiscal consequences of design, density, service patterns, and infrastructure choices. My thanks to Kevin for generously reviewing the final manuscript, offering thoughtful feedback, and for becoming a trusted colleague and friend.

Equally influential has been Ryan Short and CivicBrand, whose approach reframes community engagement as trust-building work. He has helped reshape how I think about helping communities grapple honestly with cost, trade-offs, and responsibility. I'm incredibly grateful to Ryan for being a source of encouragement from the very beginning. He was among the first to tell me this book needed to exist. His belief in the work and guidance throughout the publication process helped carry this project to completion. I'm thankful for the friendship we have forged.

This book was also shaped by the communities and colleagues I had the privilege to work for and alongside throughout my career at the Champaign (IL) Park District, the City of Bloomington (IN), and the City of Boulder (CO). Each place left a mark. From dedicated professionals who modeled excellence and care for public service, I learned what it looks like to commit to something larger than yourself. From difficult moments and imperfect systems, I learned about the cost of poor decisions and the danger of avoidance. Those lessons remain with me and echo throughout these pages.

To the readers of the first drafts, Neal Ames, Tatiana Crisan, Jill Nunes, and Geneva Slupski, thank you for sitting with the rough, vulnerable beginnings of this manuscript. Your willingness to engage with ideas that were still finding their footing strengthened the spine of this work. And to Janine Hegarty, thank you for lending your time, intellect, editorial lens, and generosity to the final shaping of this book. Your ability to illuminate gaps in thinking sharpened the book's clarity.

To my mentors, Sara Hensley and Michal Anne Lord, you have been steadying forces throughout my career. You offered challenge wrapped in grace, hard truths delivered with compassion, and wisdom shaped by experience and integrity. You have modeled what principled public service looks like when the stakes are high, the terrain is rough, and the path is uncertain. Your influence has shaped not only how I exhibit leadership, but who I strive to be. I am forever grateful.

To the 110% team I am privileged to work alongside, Matt David, Alexis Rankey, and Farrell Buller, this book is, in many ways, a reflection of what we have built together.

Matt, our utility player, your willingness to step into any role, shoulder any task, and quietly hold our work together is essential to all we do. You bring steadiness, humility, and an uncommon work ethic that keeps our projects moving forward even when the path isn't clear. Your fingerprints are on nearly every project we deliver, and nothing we produce reaches its full potential without your persistence, care, and quiet determination to make things better.

Alexis, our data sage, you have a rare ability to translate complexity into clarity. Numbers and systems that overwhelm others somehow become understandable in your hands. Your discernment and rigor keep our work honest and grounded in reality, reminding us that good intentions must always be matched by honest analysis. And just as importantly, your dry wit and thoughtful perspective keep all of us grounded when the work feels heavy.

Farrell, our "sunshine," you have been a trusted colleague and friend for many years. Even when we chose different professional paths for a time, I think we both knew we would eventually find our way back to working together. Your strength, intelligence, and joy bring possibility to each day. You have a remarkable way of seeing opportunity where others see obstacles, and your presence reminds all of us that meaningful work can still be filled with laughter and optimism. I am deeply grateful that our paths realigned.

To my sister, Judy, you have walked beside me longer than anyone. Through all that shaped us, you have remained a constant source in my life. Thank you for always being there.

To my daughter Maddy and son Mason, you have been quiet companions on this journey in ways you may not yet fully realize. You read early and final drafts not only as reviewers, but as the next generation who will inherit the consequences of the choices we make today. Your curiosity, intelligence, and growing sense of the world remind me daily why this work matters. If this book accomplishes anything, I hope it helps inspire the creation of communities worthy of your futures.

To my wife, Lisa, there are not enough pages in any book to capture the depth of my gratitude. You read more drafts than I could count. You listened to half-formed arguments, challenged me when I needed it, and steadied me through the long stretches of writing and revision. Thank you for standing with me through the ordinary and demanding moments of everyday life, and for believing in me when I struggle to believe in myself. You remind me that nothing has to be shouldered alone. I'm better because of you.

And to my Mom, I miss you and carry you with me each and every day. I hope my work and this book would have made you proud.

FURTHER READINGS AND FOUNDATIONS

This book is grounded in practice, experience, and difficult choices made in real communities under real constraints. It is not intended to be comprehensive or academic. Still, no work like this emerges in isolation.

The resources below reflect thinkers, practitioners, and institutions that have shaped our understanding of public finance, civic leadership, community design, infrastructure stewardship, and the ethical responsibilities of government. They are offered as pathways for those who wish to explore the deeper foundations behind the ideas presented in this book.

Some are practical. Some are provocative. All, in different ways, wrestle with the same core question: *How do communities endure?*

Fiscal Stewardship & Public Finance

How values, money, and long-term responsibility intersect in public systems.

Strong Towns – Charles L. Marohn Jr.

A clear and accessible critique of growth-at-all-costs thinking, with a focus on long-term fiscal resilience, infrastructure obligations, and incremental, people-centered investment.

The Price of Government – David Osborne & Peter Hutchinson

A practical framework for aligning public spending with outcomes, priorities, and community values rather than historical habit.

Government Finance Officers Association (GFOA) Best Practices

Applied guidance on budgeting, capital planning, financial policies, and transparency—where stewardship meets implementation.

Public Budgeting Systems – Robert D. Lee et al.

Foundational context for how public budgets are constructed, constrained, and managed in the real world.

<u>Place, Power & the Built Environment</u>

How decisions about land, infrastructure, and authority shape civic life.

The Civic Brand — Ryan Short

A modern exploration of civic identity, trust, and engagement, emphasizing the role of narrative, clarity, and authenticity in public institutions.

The Death and Life of Great American Cities — Jane Jacobs

A foundational work on human-scale cities, community vitality, and the unintended consequences of top-down planning.

The Power Broker — Robert A. Caro

A cautionary examination of power and decision-making, illustrating how public works can shape—or distort—communities when accountability is absent

For the Love of Cities — Peter Kageyama

A exploration of how emotional connection to place drives civic pride, engagement, and care.

Leadership, Governance & Decision-Making

Why good intentions fail and what holds when pressure rises.

Team of Rivals — Doris Kearns Goodwin

A powerful study of Abraham Lincoln's leadership, illustrating humility, restraint, moral clarity, and the capacity to govern effectively amid deep division.

Leadership on the Line — Ronald Heifetz & Marty Linsky

A core text on adaptive leadership, particularly when technical fixes are insufficient, and values conflict.

The Fifth Discipline — Peter Senge

Systems thinking applied to organizations, emphasizing learning, feedback loops, and long-term consequences.

Governing for the Long Term — ICMA resources

Applied insights on balancing political realities with ethical stewardship and institutional continuity.

<u>Ethics, Trust & the Public Obligation</u>

The moral responsibilities behind public decisions

Ethics in Public Administration — Patrick J. Sheeran

Ethical frameworks for public servants navigating competing interests and limited resources.

Trust in Government Research — Pew Research Center

Data-driven insight into declining trust and the conditions under which it can be rebuilt.

ABOUT THE AUTHOR

Jamie Sabbach is the founder and president of 110% Inc., a consulting and education firm specializing in fiscal stewardship and responsible decision-making in local government. A sought-after speaker, facilitator, and educator, she has presented nationally and internationally and has testified before the U.S. Congress on the importance of parks, recreation, and other quality-of-life services.

Jamie works with elected officials, executive teams, and practitioners across the country to help them navigate complexity, confront hard trade-offs, and align public investment with public purpose. Her work sits at the intersection of math, meaning, and leadership—emphasizing clarity over comfort, long-term responsibility over short-term wins, and courage over convenience. Known for blending practical financial frameworks with values-based leadership and plain-spoken storytelling, she helps organizations move from aspiration to accountability while protecting the services and places that shape community quality of life.

www.ingramcontent.com/pod-product-compliance
Ingram Content Group UK Ltd.
Pitfield, Milton Keynes, MK11 3LW, UK
UKHW021937190726
13853UKWH00004B/1496

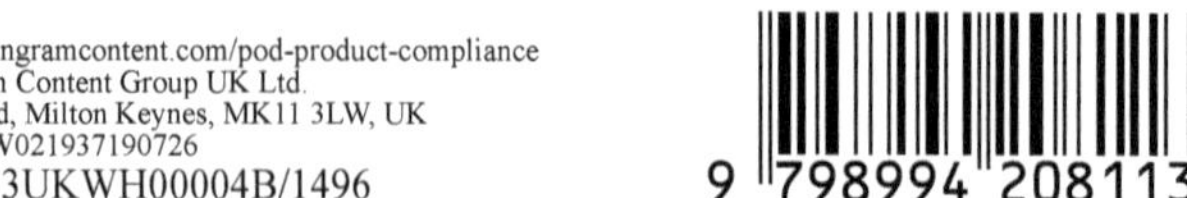

9 798994 208113